THE AMERICAN MOVIE

BOOKS BY
WILLIAM K. EVERSON
THE WESTERN, 1962
NICKELODEON DAYS, 1962

EVERETT AISON
ARTHUR, 1961, ILLUSTRATOR

WRITTEN BY WILLIAM K. EVERSON   DESIGNED BY EVERETT AISON   ATHENEUM, 1963, NEW YORK

THE AMERICAN MOVIE   THE AMERICAN MOVIE   THE AMERICAN MOVIE

THE AMERICAN MOVIE   THE AMERICAN MOVIE   THE AMERICAN MOVIE

THE AMERICAN MOVIE   THE AMERICAN MOVIE   THE AMERICAN MOVIE

To BETTY BRONSON. One of the loveliest stars of the movies' gentlest years.

This book is in no way intended as a comprehensive history of the movies. It is instead an introductory survey of American film history, dealing in general terms with the film pioneers, the great film landmarks, the technological changes through the years, and the different trends and cycles the movies have undergone.

Those interested in film history and/or film art today have a great advantage over those seeking information only ten years ago. Today there is a renewed interest in, and availability of, films of the past. Almost all of the films of the thirties are to be seen again, either in the theater or on television. Even many of the great silents have been revived. Most of the pictures mentioned in this book can be seen again today; not always easily it's true; but they are there.

However, be forewarned. Television can offer a distorted view of films of the past. Many are so badly cut to fit into pre-planned time slots that they are hardly representative of their original versions. Too, television is a great leveller—the good films seem much less good, and the bad films often seem much better than they are. A very talkative, static stage adaptation may seem good just because it is by its very nature well suited to the television screen. And a cheaply made film can have its cheapness hidden by the small screen. Conversely, the merits of a huge spectacle film, or one noted for its camera work, may be almost lost when the small television screen distorts and changes the original image. Certain comedies which depend on the steadily building laughter of a large audience and are paced to allow time for that laughter, seem curiously flat and unfunny on television. Participating audience reaction is often quite as important an ingredient as a key performance or outstanding photography.

So, if you study films on television, form your own opinions, but if a much praised film disappoints you, be prepared to withhold a final judgment until you can see it on a movie screen.

CONTENTS

THE AMERICAN MOVIE

It's astonishing to look back and think that one hundred years ago, seventy five even, there were no movies at all. Probably no other form of art or entertainment has ever made so much progress in so short a time.

There were books of a sort from earliest times. But it was centuries before the printing press made books available to everyone. The wheel is often considered the single most important invention of all. But thousands of years went by between the discovery of the wheel and the coming of the first automobile at the turn of this century.

The motion picture of course did not develop out of nothing. Basically movies are a series of still pictures projected on a screen and given the illusion of movement by means of a machine. The pictures tell a story, and since the late 1920's have been accompanied by sound, both voice and music. Pictures, even great art work, have been with us since the beginning of human civilization. Great stories, great literature, music, plays, and fine acting go back to the ancient Greeks and even before. None of this was like the movies, however. They could not come until science developed the electric light, photography, and the phonograph.

When these had been invented, they were combined with the earlier art forms and a completely new art came into being, one that in the late 1890's nobody dreamed could exist. The movies

The light-truck used in
photographing the New York Subway
opening in 1904

then were new, and seemed to be a novelty, a passing fancy that would have no practical use in business, nor any great value for education or culture. Yet within a mere twenty years of their first appearance, the movies had not only become a gigantic business all over the world, but were in some cases permanent works of art.

Of course, in the early days, the very early days, from 1898 to about 1903, little was great. The movies were still just a novelty. It was enough that they moved. That they tell stories or convey important ideas seemed unnecessary. So they showed news events of the day, fashions, the opening of the new subway in New York City. And in so doing they provided an invaluable historical record of America at a time when it was undergoing great changes.

Apart from these "newsreels," there were other "entertainment" items. These were simple little comedies that ran for only a few minutes: a boy playing pranks on his teacher, a woman who could not stop laughing after an overdose of laughing gas from her dentist, and that sort of thing.

If the movies had done only these things and stopped, the new invention would not have lasted very long. But many of the men working in films were artists with vision and imagination. And through them the movies rapidly became more and more impressive.

One of the first of these great pioneers was a Frenchman, George Méliès. He realized that the movies had a certain magic quality to them and made use of it. He played with film the way a magician plays with his magic hat; experiment showed that he could do all kinds of tricks. Just by photographing a man sitting in a chair, stopping the camera for a moment, removing the man, and then rephotographing the empty chair, one could create an absolutely convincing illusion of a man vanishing into thin air.

From 1902 on, Méliès made hundreds of astonishingly good trick films—the first science fiction films for example, with a rocket ship trip to the moon. So cunningly and expertly were these trick films made, that his pictures even today delight audiences lucky enough to see them. Today, of course, we know how the tricks were done, but audiences of 1902 did not. Movies were still so new that a simple shot of a train thundering along the tracks and looking as though it were going to run right over the audience was enough to cause a near panic. So rocket ships, monsters, underwater scenes (Méliès made the first version of Jules Verne's *20,000 Leagues Under the Sea*) were magic indeed. And it was this kind of magic and excitement that began to build the movies into something far more than a novelty.

Trick films alone could not keep the movies going and growing, of course. And they did not. Other things happened. Films

Luckily, just when the movies needed him most, one man came along with ideas. He brought "grammar" to film, along with a lot of other unheard-of ideas. Almost overnight he turned the movies from a novelty into an art, and made films which are still regarded as some of the finest made anywhere at any time. He not only made great films, but he also taught others how to make them. Any film that you see anywhere today has something in it that originated with this one man, David Wark Griffith.

picture or why they were doing what they were. The audience understood the story, but there was nothing to make the story seem really exciting.

The problem was that the director, the most important man in the making of a film—the man who tells the actors how to act, the cameraman where to put his camera, and who decides which scene will be short and which one long—was still little more than a traffic policeman. He waved his arms to start the scene going, waved them again to stop it, and that was all. He wasn't "punctuating" the film. Most of the time the camera was in one fixed position, usually quite a way away from the action so that all of the actors could be seen at the same time. Sometimes this sort of a shot is a good one, but used constantly it is dull and keeps the audience from understanding some of the action. Is the heroine happy or sad about a turn of events? The audience doesn't know because it can't see the emotions on her face.

To make matters worse, the audience seldom knew what was happening elsewhere in the story. Today, if robbers are breaking in, we expect to know that the police are on their way and to be left wondering if they will arrive on time. We find this exciting. In early films, the police arrived just at the right moment, but no one knew they were coming. This finished off the story neatly enough, but it didn't provide much drama.

Filming a boxing match: 1898

grew longer. By 1903 it became fairly common for the "main feature" of the bill to run for a full reel, or about 12 minutes. This was a great advance.

That year another great pioneer, Edwin S. Porter, who was the leading film-maker for the Thomas A. Edison Studios in West Orange, New Jersey, made a film called *The Great Train Robbery.* It was the first real western adventure story, and in a way was the blueprint for all the westerns that were to come. It set the pattern of crime—pursuit—and capture. Western stories at once became tremendously popular with movie-makers, even though the New Jersey and New York landscapes, where all movies were then made, didn't really suggest the Wild West.

The most important companies in those early years were Edison (New Jersey), and Vitagraph (Brooklyn). In addition to westerns, these studios made short thrillers, romances, and adaptations of classic literature. But something seemed to be missing. It wasn't the photography, which was surprisingly expert. And it wasn't the stories, which in many cases were good. What was lacking was a kind of "grammar" of film. Seeing a movie was like reading a story without any punctuation. The story began and went on without any stops or starts or exclamations to emphasize the important or exciting parts. In addition the audience never learned much about the people in the

Edison's
Black Maria Studio

Shooting inside the first
Biograph Studios
at 841 Broadway, New York

Tunnelling the English Channel (Melies)

THE FORMULATIVE YEARS

Griffith made his first film, *The Adventure Of Dollie,* for Biograph, and he made it reluctantly. He had been a stage actor, was employed by Biograph as an actor, and had no interest in directing. But he was persuaded to do so; and for a man who knew nothing about film, his first showed an amazing ability.

The picture is a simple, melodramatic story of a child kidnapped by gypsies. She is placed in a barrel, the barrel falls into a river, and she is carried over a small waterfall—to emerge unharmed and be reunited with her worried parents. Griffith told the entire story without titles, the written explanations used in silent pictures. He kept his action in the outdoors; the scenes were short, and the action swift. The result was a more polished film than those being made by "veterans" who had been turning them out for five years and more.

Griffith was soon persuaded by the Biograph Company to continue directing pictures. The company was a small one located at 11 East 14th Street in New York City. Its earlier movies had sometimes been good, but the general run of its product was mediocre. The company was no competition for the bigger studios like Vitagraph and Edison. Apart from the overall good quality of their photography, due to the capabilities of their chief cameraman G. W. "Billy" Bitzer, there was little to distinguish the firm from the dozens of other small

film companies mushrooming on the East Coast.

The whole mechanism of film production was simpler then, and there was room and opportunity for many companies. As soon as a picture was completed (and they never ran more than a single reel, with a running time of about 12 minutes) it was advertised and sold outright to exhibitors and distributors at so much per foot. The physical print then belonged to the purchaser, to be used for as long as it remained in runnable condition. There were no "rights" by which a film produced by a company could be protected from unlawful exhibition or copying. It was not even possible to copyright motion pictures until 1912; before that they came under the heading of "photographs." Many dealers made a practice of buying up good films, making inferior copies, and putting their own trademarks on them. Eventually the leading studios were able to put a stop to this practice by placing their own trademarks prominently on the wall in important scenes.

Griffith came onto the scene in 1908, and by late 1909 he had completely learned the mechanics of film making and was ready to apply his own imagination. That year he produced two gems. One was *A Corner In Wheat,* a remarkable and daring picture dealing with stock manipulation. It finished with the corrupt financial genius being drowned in a pit of his own grain and the poverty-stricken farmers facing the future hopelessly. Beautifully photographed by Bitzer, it was a film Griffith obviously cared about. He spent ten days shooting it. (One-hour westerns in the thirties were sometimes turned out in three days!)

That same year, Griffith made a film called *The Lonely Villa*. This exciting melodrama was one of the first films featuring Mary Pickford, who later became one of the great stars of the silent movies. In this film for the first time Griffith began to explore seriously the tension-building possibilities of editing and cross-cutting. He showed the family bidding the father farewell, while desperate burglars wait to break in. The father gone, the burglars arrive. By a ruse, one of them empties the gun that the father has left for his family's protection. As the men gain entrance, the mother and three daughters barricade themselves in a room. That door gives way, and the besieged women escape to another room. Meanwhile, the father's car has broken down. He stops at an inn and telephones his wife. She has just time to tell him of their predicament before one of the thugs cuts the phone wires. The burglars continue their assault. Father is desperate; the car cannot be repaired, but he finds a gypsy encampment. He commandeers a horse and wagon, and with police, rushes to the rescue. The tempo increases now, as Griffith cuts between the frightened women and the wagon bringing help. Burglars and police break in at the same moment, and we have the first of Griffith's last-minute rescues. If this seems common now, remember that in 1909 such cutting had not been used at all.

From *The Lonely Villa,* Griffith took another step forward in *The Lonedale Operator* of 1911. Here a telegraph operator is trying to protect the payroll from bandits. The hero is rushing to her aid in a locomotive. The pattern is the same, but the treatment is more polished. There is faster cutting and better use of the camera, which in some scenes is placed in the cab of the engine and in others at an extremely low angle by the side of the tracks. Too, the characterization is more developed: Blanche Sweet, as the heroine, is given seemingly "unnecessary" little bits of business and byplay, so that one feels she is a genuine person. Even the villains are rather likeable; and at the end, when one of them finds that they have been tricked by the heroine's cunning, he pays his tribute to her with a courtly bow.

Griffith liked this story so much that he remade it again in 1912 as *A Girl and Her Trust.* The new picture shows an astonishing gain in style in only one year. This time the bandits do get in, grab the payroll, and try to make an escape on a handcar, taking the heroine with them. The hero is in hot pursuit in the locomotive. Griffith loaded his camera on an automobile running along a road parallel to the railroad tracks, and also

onto another locomotive running just in front of the one manned by his hero. This one element added a fantastic amount of excitement and speed, especially for audiences that had never seen it done before. Griffith was the foremost pioneer in this use of the moving camera. The technique did not come into really widespread use until the mid 1920's.

Not all of Griffith's films were chase melodramas, of course. He made adaptations of literary classics, ranging from James Fenimore Cooper to Charles Dickens; he made several films attacking social evils (drunkenness, drug addiction, etc.) and he was outspoken in his attacks on bigotry, greed, and intolerance. He made charming little romances with Mary Pickford, Lillian Gish, and Mae Marsh. These were all the more effective because Griffith taught his actors the value of "underplaying" a scene. He brought his cameras close to the players so that they could express emotion by a lowered eyelid or a tightening of the lips. It was said of him that he "photographed thought"— and it was true.

From 1910 on, Griffith took his unit to California every winter to take advantage of the better weather, and there he produced some marvellous westerns. *The Last Drop Of Water* (1911) is a poetic and exciting tale of covered wagon days. *Fighting Blood, The Massacre,* and *The Battle Of Elderbush Gulch* (all 1911–13) were outstanding Indian-vs-cavalry west-

erns, containing large scale battle scenes, tense last-minute rescues, panoramic vistas of action, and well-used closeups.

While Griffith was pioneering and exploring, surprisingly few of the other directors were taking advantage of the lessons he was teaching. He was so much ahead of his time that his methods were not fully understood except by the men who worked with him. But there was one man who for a while was a serious rival to Griffith and in the early days was one of the most important film-makers. His name was Thomas H. Ince, and like Griffith he was a former actor who had drifted into directing almost accidentally.

Ince, too, favored melodramas, especially westerns and Civil War stories. His approach however was quite different. Griffith cared little for story; style and technique were what put his films over. Very often his "plot" was little more than a single situation milked for every last drop of suspense. Ince didn't concern himself with editing. He wanted story, with characterization and well-staged action. His exciting battle scenes and Indian fights were beautifully done and completely convincing. And he liked the value of a shock ending. Many of his films came to unexpectedly tragic endings, sometimes simply because it was the most honest way out. And audiences did not mind. Movies were still short and those who watched had little time to build up a real feeling for the hero. This was the time before the establishment of big stars and no one as yet had any real favorites. So there was no feeling of sadness or disappointment when a player like Tom Chatterton was killed off in the climax.

Ince maintained a high standard, but unlike Griffith, he didn't develop. There is little difference between an Ince western of 1910 and one of 1913. Too, he himself directed only in the early phases of his career. By 1913 he had given up personal direction in favor of supervision. He trained and discovered other directors, kept close personal touch with the films they made, but was not a creative artist in himself. However, he liked to *think* that he was, and he usually inserted a "Directed by Thomas H. Ince" credit on every film that turned out well, whether it was directed by Francis Ford, William S. Hart, Reginald Barker or any one of a dozen other directors in his employ.

For all of this, Ince was an extremely able film-maker. It was he who created the job of "production supervisor," later an essential figure in all top studios. He worked out efficient and quick methods of shooting; and it was Ince who pioneered the detailed shooting script. Ince's scripts, with each shot broken down carefully, gave instructions to the carpenters as to what the sets should look like, told the cameramen which angles to use, advised on which scenes should be shot first, and even gave

the laboratories notes as to which scenes should be tinted amber, which pink, and so on. A final note of preparedness: the scripts even contained dialogue (in addition to the printed titles) so that the actors would have a full understanding of their roles and would know what to say, even though there would be no sound recorded.

Griffith used no scripts at all; Ince used extremely elaborate ones. Each found that his own method paid off well for himself. It is significant, however, that a far greater number of fine stars and directors emerged under Griffith's "instinctive" methods than under the more organized, assembly-line tactics of Ince.

Ince's career after 1913 did not keep pace with Griffith's. He continued to be active for many years, but mainly by using the two important stars he had built up—William S. Hart and Charles Ray. His importance dwindled, and he died in the mid-1920's.

By 1912 the industry was undergoing the first of what became regular upheavals. This time it was started by the coming of feature-length films. No one is quite sure when the first feature was made. Claims have been made for both *The Squaw Man* by Cecil B. DeMille and Griffith's *Judith of Bethulia*. Actually, features of five and six reels were fairly common at least a year before these two pictures appeared. Most of the early features were bad. The scripts had little real content and were no more than padded stories that should have been told in two reels. The approach was stagey, as if the movies were trying to duplicate the theater. There was little or no film grammar, no acknowledgement of the lessons that Griffith had taught. But audiences seemed unaware of these shortcomings; it was enough that these early features were of long duration.

Griffith realized that this could not go on. Good features would have to be made, or the industry could be ruined. He begged his employers to let him make features, to put to full use in them all the innovations and ideas he had developed. The company finally allowed him to make the four-reel *Judith Of Bethulia;* but when it was finished, Biograph was afraid of it (though it was far better than the features that had already proved themselves acceptable to audiences) and held back its release.

Feeling that he could get nowhere with the over-cautious Biograph, Griffith left for the now rapidly mushrooming Hollywood, taking with him the cameraman Bitzer and a number of key stars. Biograph, without his genius, struggled along for a few more years, and then went bankrupt: a tragic ending for a company that had been such a leader for so many years.

In Hollywood, Griffith joined the Reliance-Majestic Company. There he spent a year turning out pictures just to meet

payrolls and keep the company in business until he was ready to move ahead. Considering the rushed conditions under which many of these movies were made, and the fact that they were produced simply to make money, the standards Griffith achieved were incredible. Some of the two-reelers made under his supervision, and *The Doll House Mystery* was one of the best, were not only excellent films but showed how well directors under his guidance were absorbing his teachings.

Griffith himself made several features. One of them, *The Avenging Conscience,* was a unique experiment in filming Edgar Allan Poe. Although the picture seems a little crude and obvious in some ways today, it was a remarkable accomplishment then. The suspense and feeling of underlying horror he achieved were hailed by knowing critics as a supreme accomplishment. However, good as this film was, it was soon to be totally overshadowed. For in 1915 and 1916 D. W. Griffith unveiled two masterpieces of American film-making. To explain the impact of these two pictures is like trying to explain the concept and teachings of the Bible to someone who has never read it. For these two films were to become almost the Bible of movies. They were *The Birth of a Nation* and its successor, *Intolerance.*

An Unseen Enemy: Lillian and Dorothy Gish
One of Griffith's best suspense stories (1912)

Griffith and Bitzer photographing **Intolerance**

THE FIRST MASTERPIECES

When *The Birth of a Nation* exploded on the screen, first in Los Angeles at Clune's Auditorium on February 8, 1915, and later in New York at the Liberty Theater on March 3, 1915, audiences were stunned. It was the longest film yet made, for one thing, running for three hours. But more than that, it was such a dynamic piece of work that all the good films that had come before—and there had been some very good ones—now seemed like fumblings in the dark.

The Birth of a Nation was divided into two parts. The bulk of the first half dealt with events leading up to and including the Civil War. The surrender of Lee, the assassination of Lincoln, and some truly monumental battle scenes were pictured. The last half of the film shows the effects on the South of Reconstruction, the exploitation of the newly-freed Negroes by industrialists and politicians from the North, and the ways in which the South tried to reestablish order.

Financed by private backers, *The Birth of a Nation* cost $110,000. By today's standards, that is a trifling sum. But in 1915 it was a fantastic amount, over five times greater than any other sum spent on a single movie. More important than the money itself was the fact that it showed just how much faith Griffith had in the future of the motion picture. Those who thought he was mad to spend so much and make such a long film had to admit they were wrong when overnight it

Henry B. Walthall
"The Little Colonel" of
The Birth of a Nation

brought new respect for the entire industry. It also established the movies as very much of a big business.

The picture became the biggest boxoffice success of all times. Because of the haphazard way it was financed and sold, nobody knows just how much the film has made through the years, and still continues to make. But it is known that it has earned a minimum of fifty million dollars.

Audiences were overwhelmed by Griffith's technique. He would "iris in" his camera to film a love scene, giving it the quaint charm of an old Daguerrotype. As horsemen thundered across the screen, he would mask off the top and bottom of the picture to give a long, wide picture, just as today's Cinema-Scope does. He took his camera back, or up into the air, to take in vast panoramas of action. He mounted his camera on a truck and got right in front of galloping horses to shoot close-ups of the riders or the horses' hooves. He would build up to a climax, relax, and then build the tension all over again. For his final climax, he had two groups of people in steadily increasing danger—with rescue on the way—and cut back and forth between the two. Audiences who had only a glimpse of this kind of film grammar in earlier Griffith films were caught in the grip of feverish excitement. The story was thrilling in itself, but the way it was told increased their reaction. They were caught up without knowing why.

Similarly, the audience came to accept the film's political and historical arguments. So persuasive was the arrangement of shots that audiences didn't realize that the editing was selling them ideas as well as entertainment. No matter what issues are at stake, there are two sides to every question. But Griffith, here, was only concerned with one side—the Southern side—and so dynamic was the way he presented it that the onlooker felt there could be no other interpretation of the facts. And therein lay the basis for many criticisms of the film.

It is, of course, possible to present on the screen (or in literature) a "surface" truth that is actually far from the truth; and Griffith's film was accused of this many times. The fact that a dozen law suits failed to prove the inaccuracy of *The Birth of a Nation* by no means put an end to the accusations. The stories went on and on that Griffith nursed anti-Negro feelings that prejudiced his treatment of history.

Griffith can be accused of treating the Negroes with condescension, but not with hostility. On the contrary, he went out of his way to be fair to the Negro, and to place the blame for most of their errors squarely on the shoulders of white politicians. Perhaps, however, President Woodrow Wilson (from whose book *The History of the American People* Griffith took many of his facts) summed it up best when he endorsed the film wholeheartedly with this statement:

"It is like writing history with lightning. My one regret is that it is all so terribly true."

Certainly no finer film on the War Between the States has ever been made. It would be possible to remove all of the story from the film and be left with a remarkable history of the War: the years before, the years after, and the passing of a way of life in the South.

As a historical spectacle, and as an artistic triumph, *The Birth of a Nation* could have stood unchallenged for years. It would have been a fitting climax to any career. But for Griffith it was just the beginning, and within a year, it was overshadowed by a film that Griffith made almost accidentally— *Intolerance*.

Griffith had been working on a powerful but not too ambitious film called *The Mother and the Law*. It was a modern story of a man wrongly convicted of murder, and attacked intolerance in modern society. But then came the controversy over *The Birth of a Nation*. Griffith was hurt and appalled at the way his film was misunderstood; and he was angry at the so-called reformers and crusaders who tried to inflict their views on others. He decided to expand *The Mother and the Law* into a much more elaborate film that would show the results of oppression and injustice through the ages, with religious, political, and social tyranny as his main targets. He

Lillian Gish

Mae Marsh in the modern sequence of **Intolerance**

Griffith directing **Intolerance**

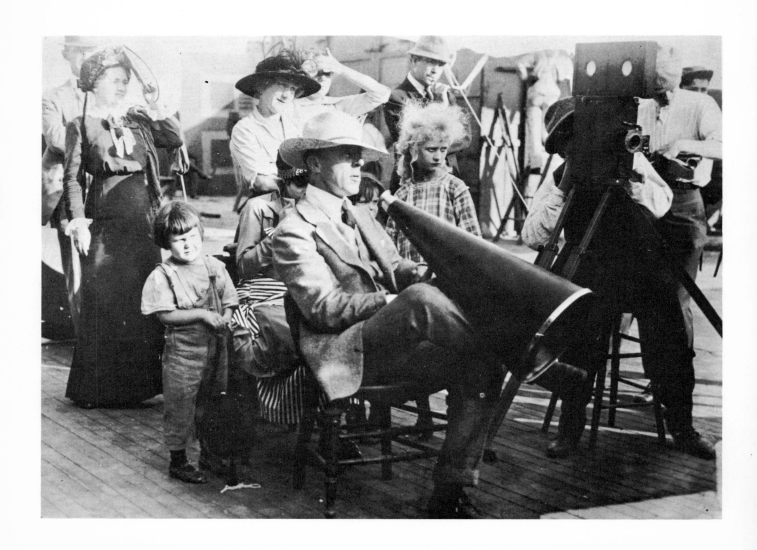

Sherman's March to the Sea from **The Birth of a Nation**

told his modern story and added to it one of the overthrow of Babylon by Cyrus the Persian, one dealing with religious persecution in France during the reign of Catherine de Medici, and the story of Christ and his crucifixion.

The film begins in a leisurely way, establishing its periods, introducing its characters, and staying with each story for a considerable length of time. The stories are told in parallel sequence, cutting from one period to another, one character to another. As the young mother in the modern story is deprived of her child by hypocritical reformers, there is a quick cut to another age—to Christ surrounded by loving children, and the title "Suffer little children to come unto me." But the real unification of themes is introduced in the latter portions of the three-hour film when each story is approaching its climax—the execution of the hero in the modern story, the fall of Babylon, the St. Bartholomew's massacre, and the crucifixion of Christ.

As the depths of mankind's cruelties and ills from religious, political, and personal intolerance increase, Griffith gradually increases the tempo of his cutting. It goes from a long shot of chariots racing to a long shot of a speeding locomotive; close-up from one story to close-up in another. And amazingly, this most complex of all cutting patterns was not planned on paper or even executed mechanically. Griffith conceived and produced this whole production without any kind of script or

Crowd scene
from **Intolerance**

written notes to guide his editing.

In terms of audience appeal its Babylonian sequence—now as then—comes off best. For sheer spectacle, it has never been equalled. The sets, the magnificent organization of the huge crowd scenes, the incredibly realistic and savage battle scenes, still take one's breath away. In the massive mob scenes, Griffith had several assistant directors concealed, directing individual segments of action. Griffith's mob scenes were always superbly controlled; with unerring instinct, he directed the spectator's eye to the action he wanted noticed. Too, the extras weren't just a surging mob. They look desperate, afraid, angry; one will nudge another; one here will help defend a comrade. They perform as individuals, not as part of a mob, and this is what always made Griffith's crowd scenes so completely realistic. Current spectacles are minor-league both in size and in artistry compared with this work of so long ago.

In spite of the superb crowds, however, it is the modern sequence, without spectacle, that is strongest dramatically. It had a lasting effect on film-makers, influencing directors from Fred Niblo and John Ford in the U. S. A. to Eisenstein and Pudovkin in Russia.

Photographically the film is a triumph, and a remarkable advance even on *The Birth of a Nation*. Amazingly, most of the picture was shot with a single small hand-cranked camera. The moving camera is used tastefully and to good dramatic effect. None of the huge streamlined camera cranes of today could better the results achieved by Griffith and his cameraman G. W. Bitzer with their simple equipment and "do-it-yourself" camera crane that was pushed back and forth on railroad tracks.

Although *The Birth of a Nation* had been an immediate popular success, *Intolerance* was not. With its fantastically complex construction, it exhausted 1916 audiences. They were shattered by its power, worn out by its tempo, and they just did not understand the idea behind it. Audiences today no longer fail to understand it, but it remains an unavoidably exhausting film to sit through.

It goes without saying that in 1916 *Intolerance* was a box-office flop. Even releasing the modern story and the Babylonian story later as separate features didn't enable Griffith to recoup his losses.

It is difficult to determine the film's cost, but it is generally considered to have been about two million dollars. This is a fairly common sum for movies today, but it was an unheard of amount in 1916. However, in 1934, G. W. Bitzer estimated that to remake it then, with no changes other than the addition of a simple sound track (but taking into consideration all the added production costs, much higher star salaries, union rates, and so

on), would cost fifteen million dollars. Ten years later, another re-evaluation put a remake cost at thirty million dollars. In the sixties when *Ben Hur* allegedly cost sixteen million dollars and *Mutiny on the Bounty* and *Cleopatra* both well above twenty million, no one could say what a new *Intolerance* would take.

Fortunately, *Intolerance,* which is considered to be America's foremost film masterpiece, is the kind of film that cannot be remade. It is complete and perfect as it is—as complete and perfect as a Rembrandt painting or a Bach cantata. It has been called the only film fugue.

Griffith, with all the great films that he made in after years, never again did anything so fine as *Intolerance*. Nor has anyone else.

The Birth of a Nation

The four years from 1916 to 1920 form one of the most enjoyable periods in film history. Yet, strangely, it is a period that is seldom talked about. Perhaps this is because there were no real "landmarks" in those years. There were many very good films and a handful of excellent ones, but none with the strength and influence of *The Birth of a Nation*. Historians like to deal in dates and "development," and so they jump from *Intolerance* in 1916 to Germany's *The Cabinet of Dr. Caligari* in 1919, and from there to the twenties.

For much of this four year period, America was at war with Germany; but it was a war that was being fought three thousand miles away. Those at home bought war bonds, and women replaced men as mail deliverers. It all seemed rather exciting, and few sacrifices had to be made. The realities of war and its horrors were somehow lost. The newsreels helped in this rather complacent feeling. There were few scenes shown of actual battle. The stress was placed instead on training: on the men in camps singing, playing, being entertained, all happy, healthy and eager to get into the fray. The movies *about* the war were, for the most part, wild spy melodramas, thrillers that were little more than glorified westerns or overdone propaganda films which showed the crimes of the "beastly Hun." These crimes were usually directed against the helpless French and Belgian peasants; hence American audiences could rise in in-

dignation, rush out and buy more war bonds, and yet feel little anxiety for the American forces.

Perhaps only one really serious and honest film about the war was made during the war itself—D. W. Griffith's *Hearts of the World*. It was made in France, often under fire, at the request of the British government. Had Griffith made it a little sooner, or had the war lasted longer, it would have brought home to the American people the *true* horror of war and the absence of glory. But shortly after the film was finished, the war itself came to a close. Audiences wanted to forget the war; if they were to see it on the screen at all, they wanted to be able to laugh at it as Charlie Chaplin had done in his *Shoulder Arms*. So *Hearts of the World*, which could well have become one of the most important films of its era, went largely unseen. Its anti-war theme is a timeless one and today the film is still powerful and effective; but in 1918, it was unwanted.

The wartime propaganda films apart, the movies of 1916–1920 were not trying to "persuade" or "teach" audiences about anything. They had one simple idea: to entertain. How could they best entertain? Be funny, be thrilling, be appealing, be friendly. In fact, the word "friendly" seems to sum up best the whole approach to films in that period. They were gentle; the stars were personalities that audiences could love—stars like William S. Hart, Mary Pickford and Douglas Fairbanks. It was a happy period to see pictures in—and a happy period in which to make them.

The technique of taking movies was well developed. The camera work was sharp, clear, and smooth. Many people seeing silent movies today are misled by the fast speed at which they are run into thinking that films of that period hopped and jumped about at top speed. They didn't. Apart from the deliberately speeded up action of the Mack Sennett comedies, they were shown at the normal speed of life, as are today's movies. But they were photographed at a different camera speed from today's movies and projected at a corresponding speed. When sound came in, it was necessary, for purely mechanical reasons, to increase the speed of photography and projection. As long as both remained constant, there was no difference in the speed of action on the screen. But most of today's sound projectors in theaters and TV are not equipped to run films at anything but current speeds. As a result, most of the time silents are run at almost twice the speed they were meant to be run.

Also, at this time there was really no such thing as a black-and-white film. Most silent films were printed on a variety of colored stocks; a yellow or amber would be used for sunlight scenes, blue for night, green for fog, flaming red for fire scenes, and so on. If a character turned out a light, the tone would change instantly from amber to blue. Sometimes two tones would be used, one on either side of the film. The two fused as the projection lamp shone through them. Red on one side, blue on the other, could produce an incredibly beautiful effect of a sunrise over a lake. Perfectionists like Maurice Tourneur and D. W. Griffith even had certain scenes hand painted over existing color tones. In one film, for example, Griffith hand colored a delicate pink blush on the cheek of Carol Dempster. And all of this did not call for great costs.

Movies could still be made cheaply and quickly. The mechanical problems of sound were still a long way off. With no dialogue to worry about, scripts were simple matters. Stars' salaries had not yet reached the fantastic proportions that they have today. In other words, costs were comparatively low —profits could be enormous. Because of this, there was a relaxed approach to making movies. It wasn't necessary to make "great" films; it was enough to make good ones.

In some cases, it was even enough to make just exciting ones. Nineteen fourteen had seen the birth of one of the most popular types of all, the long serial. These were ten, fifteen, or even far more, two reel chapters of fast action and mystery, each climaxed by a situation with the hero or heroine in extreme peril. Appropriately, the serials soon came to be known as "cliff-hangers." They were tremendously popular during this period and later, and often attracted far more people into the theater than the main feature.

In the beginning, as if to parallel woman's fight for social and political equality, the stars of the serials were women. Pearl White and Ruth Roland showed that anything a man could do, they could do better—whether it was riding, stunting, or landing a hefty right to the villain's jaw. In the twenties, with the vote secured, the serial queens gave over their thrones to the men, but the cliff-hangers continued their long and flourishing career.

It would be wrong to imply in all of this, however, that the films of 1916–1920 were fun but of no permanent value. On the contrary, they were of tremendous value in a great variety of ways. For one thing, they provided a valuable training ground for directors and stars, many of whom are still active today. Secondly, in their concentration on simple stories and rural themes they took their cameras out of doors and recorded an America and a way of life that is no more. Films like Lillian Gish's *True Heart Susie* (made by D. W. Griffith), Charles Ray's *The Clodhopper* and Mary Pickford's *Rebecca of Sunnybrook Farm* are invaluable today—and will be even more so in generations to come—because they show far more graphically than any history book just what America and its people were like in those days before the twenties.

Sennett's Keystone Cops
in **A Mud Bath**

Charlie Chaplin, 1916
as star-director of **The Rink**

It was in this period, too, that Hollywood's great comedy tradition came into being, starting with Mack Sennett and his wild Keystone comedies. Here Charlie Chaplin got his start, and within a few short years graduated from a crude knockabout comedian to one of the cleverest of pantomimists. In many ways, the comedies that Chaplin was making by 1917—he directed his own films, as well as starring in them—were among the best that he was ever to make. Harold Lloyd and Buster Keaton experimented and formulated their screen characters in this period, too.

Some stars never surpassed the work that they did in these years. William S. Hart, a cowboy star who loved the West and was determined to put the real West on the screen, made a score of outstanding western films between 1916 and 1920. Hart, an experienced stage actor, was already a mature man when he came to Hollywood. He knew better than anyone else what he wanted to put into his films, and so before long he was producing and directing them himself. His cowboy films were not the slick, streamlined affairs that we associate with Roy Rogers or Gene Autry. Often they were quite slow in physical action; but they were real and rugged, with an uncanny sense of period and an amazing accuracy in costuming and sets. Hart's were the first "adult" westerns in the truest sense of the word, and his best—films like *Hell's Hinges, The Aryan* and

The Testing Block—were all made before 1920.

Another star who was at his best in these early years was Douglas Fairbanks, who is remembered most for the elaborate swashbuckling adventures like *Robin Hood* that he made in the twenties. But he earned his following in these pre-1920 years when he was primarily a comedian—an intensely acrobatic one. He made two dozen films over a four year period. In almost all of them he played a happy-go-lucky modern knight possessed of all the virtues of courage and honesty, and buoyed up by a never-failing cheerfulness and a tremendous optimism. He bounded and leaped and grinned through a whole series of comedies that were not only cleverly written, but were also full of his own incredible acrobatic stunts and ingenious trick camerawork. These films had a sparkle and a sense of fun that is as lively today as it was then.

There were other stars, too, of course: Francis X. Bushman was the classic lover; Wallace Reid the more down-to-earth romantic. There were any number of fine dramatic actors like Henry B. Walthall who had graduated successfully from the stage. But stars were not made as easily then as now; stardom had to be earned, and it could only be won by the love and support of the public. The great male stars had only one female equal—Mary Pickford. More than a girl, not yet quite a woman, she was at her loveliest in these years. She tackled

drama, comedy, tragedy, melodrama, all tailored to her personality, and used the best cameramen and directors available. Like Douglas Fairbanks she is remembered more for the elaborate "specials" of the twenties; but also like him, the best of her work is to be found in these years.

D. W. Griffith was in the strange position of joining this era of innocence *after* he had shown that the movies were capable of more advanced, more adult things with *Intolerance*. But he had been ahead of his time. In 1916, audiences weren't yet ready to grow up, and *Intolerance* lost a great deal of money. To get it back and protect those who were financing him, Griffith followed the pattern of the period with such pictures as *True Heart Susie, The Girl Who Stayed at Home,* and *The Romance of Happy Valley*. Although they did not have the stature of *Intolerance,* they were fine pictures, and they represent very accurately the America of the period. But for the man who made them, they were time-killers. He was restless and wanted to move on. So did Mary Pickford, Douglas Fairbanks, and Charlie Chaplin.

Releasing their pictures through companies who could tell them what kind of films to make, these three had neither the freedom nor the money that they needed to do what they wanted to do; so, they decided to pool their resources and work together. The result was the forming in 1919 of a new com-

Mary Pickford

pany, United Artists. The first film to come from the new combine was a Fairbanks adventure, *His Majesty The American.* He hadn't changed his style much; it was still an exhilarating combination of comedy, action, and acrobatics. But the picture was a much bigger and more expensive film than any he had made before. Its story was far more complicated. It was longer. And when D. W. Griffith followed it with *Broken Blossoms*—a tender, poetic love story starring Lillian Gish and Richard Barthelmess—it was obvious that an era was over, that the movies had taken that first step from what had been a carefree childhood into an adult world.

Chaplin: **Easy Street**

Broken Blossoms: (Griffith) with Lillian Gish and Richard Barthelmess

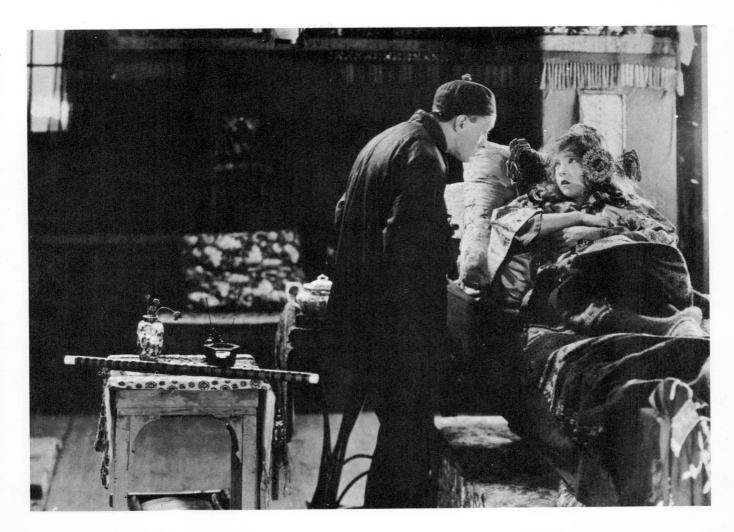

Broken Blossoms

Hell's Hinges: starring and directed by William S. Hart

THE TWENTIES

The twenties opened up with a bang. This was to be an era of expansion, of bigger and bigger pictures. Color would arrive permanently, it was predicted, and probably sound, too. The screen would "grow up" and offer more "adult" fare.

All of these things came to pass. But with the expansion also came problems. The twenties started with the control of most pictures firmly in the hands of their creators. D. W. Griffith was riding high, as head of his own company, and with his own studio. Mary Pickford, Douglas Fairbanks, William S. Hart, Buster Keaton, Charlie Chaplin, Harold Lloyd, Richard Barthelmess, Charles Ray—all were their own bosses. They made their pictures the way they wanted to, without interference from anyone.

The top directors, Erich von Stroheim, Rex Ingram, Herbert Brenon, were feted and honored. If a costly "prestige" film that one of them made lost money, the studios didn't worry unduly. Warners frequently lost money on their lavish John Barrymore costume dramas, but they knew Rin Tin Tin would always pay off the mortgage for him.

By the end of the twenties, however, it was a very different story. There was competition from radio. Production costs were going up. The bankers and the executives were insisting on control of what went into a picture to try to protect their investments from loss.

And there was another change, too—it started early in the twenties and grew rapidly. The public itself was changing. Veterans back from the war had seen too much of life to be satisfied with the kind of movies they had enjoyed a few years earlier. Even the civilians found life a letdown in the post-war years. Nor did prohibition, a law that ruled the selling of liquor illegal, help matters. Many people felt that it was an unfair intrusion on personal liberty; but it was a law. And unfortunately, it was a law that few people obeyed. With such a disregard for a governmental order, came disrespect for law in general and contempt for such qualities as patriotism. With gangsterism on the rise, the headlines told more of the exploits of bank robbers and killers than they did of Lindbergh and other happier aspects of the twenties.

The general public, of course, remained essentially law abiding. But few escaped completely the spirit of unrest and rebellion in the air. As a result the public wanted slicker, faster movies, something that matched the times. And more and more Hollywood gave in, making the same plots over and over again because studio heads knew these would succeed.

Naturally, it is only sensible to give an audience what it wants, but by the middle twenties Hollywood was overdoing it. Movie-makers had taken more than the first step in catering to the lowest tastes of the mass audience and were turning out their films like merchandise, like suits of clothes or bicycles, instead of making the best possible films and hoping that the bulk of that same mass audience would be intelligent enough to appreciate them. And events seemed to show that, in a business sense at least, this approach was right. D. W. Griffith, who did not stoop to the new trend, was one of the first movie giants to go bankrupt. His artistic presentations of great ideas seemed out of date. The public didn't want to learn about *America* in a brilliant spectacle of the Revolutionary War; they couldn't get enthused about the French Revolution in *Orphans of the Storm;* and they couldn't see why Griffith wasted their time by illustrating the evils of Communism.

Griffith, undaunted, went on making the films he thought he ought to make. He went to Germany in 1924 to make *Isn't Life Wonderful?,* a moving and compassionate story of the difficulties of refugees in post-war Europe. It was a great film, but it impressed no one—except the Germans, who the following year made *The Joyless Street* and other films patterned after it. Griffith's empire crumbled. He was forced to go to work for Paramount as a contract director, turning out the jazz-age films that the public wanted. More good work was ahead of him, but his great days were over.

Nor was Griffith the only casualty. William S. Hart was forced out of the movies in the mid-twenties. The distributors

no longer wanted his austere, poetic pictures of the old West. They wanted him to change, to become streamlined like Tom Mix. But he refused. He had one last grand fling with *Tumbleweeds,* staged a marvellous, rip-roaring reconstruction of the Cherokee Strip land rush, and retired.

Erich von Stroheim was the "wonder boy" of the early 20's. He startled audiences with his sophistication; astounded them with his fanatical attention to detail and insistence on realism; and frightened producers with the enormous sums he spent on his films. Often he shot reels and reels of film which by virtue of their very length could never arrive on the screen. As long as his films paid off at the boxoffice, as *Foolish Wives* did, nobody worried too much. But *Greed,* an intensely grim and sordid drama, was uncommercial. Others showed equal lack of potential. And as a result, few films he made after the early twenties were issued as he would have done them alone. Either they were taken away from him and finished by other directors, or they were left unfinished. By the end of the decade, he, too, had tumbled from his throne.

But if the twenties was a period of turmoil for the people who made movies, it was a period of delight for the fans who paid to see them. It was the era of the "BIG" film and the glorious adventure. Douglas Fairbanks spent millions on *The Thief of Bagdad,* and every cent showed. Its sets were huge and seemed to have been lifted right out of the *Arabian Nights*. There were trick effects, flying carpets, monsters, and marvellous fantasy. In fact, Fairbanks was so overwhelmed by his desire to produce lavish shows, that his own personality was swamped by decor and massive sets. Before the twenties were over, he realized his mistake and went back to the carefree style of an earlier time.

During the twenties Milton Sills did *The Sea Hawk,* John Barrymore made *The Sea Beast,* Rudolph Valentino was *The Son of the Sheik* and Ronald Colman was *Beau Geste.* De Mille launched a series of historical spectacles with *The Ten Commandments,* and King Vidor made one of the greatest of all war films, *The Big Parade.*

The westerns, always popular, enjoyed a whole new boom. Tom Mix, with his circus appeal, stunts, and tricks, was at the peak of his fame. His films weren't "real" and they weren't intended to be, but they were fun and packed with thrills and stunts. In 1923 James Cruze made *The Covered Wagon,* a slow moving but impressive and photographically superb western epic. Seen today, it seems rather tame, but it brought new style to the western. John Ford followed with the exciting *The Iron Horse,* and a whole flock of new cowboy stars—Fred Thomson, Ken Maynard, Bob Steele, Tom Tyler, Lane Chandler, and newcomer Gary Cooper joined the veteran favorites.

Although many fine, sincere films were made in the twenties, the dramatic classics were relatively few. The aim of all seemed to be: "Make each show bigger and better than the last." If a studio made a romance, for example, it had to be a "big" one. Some, like Frank Borzage's lovely *Seventh Heaven*—still probably one of the screen's finest love stories thanks to his sensitive treatment—were good. But "big" films could be "empty" films, too. And enough great films were being made so that the public, undiscriminating as it was, could still tell the difference just by simple comparisons.

In the old days Mary Pickford had often made four or five features a year. Now she limited herself to one, and made that a super-special. Like her husband, Douglas Fairbanks, in these big films she lost some of her sparkle and spontaneous charm. Her films became too elaborate, too big. But the stars in those days inspired genuine love and devotion from their public. The fans didn't lose faith in her because one or two pictures were disappointing. She was sure to come back with something good, and she did. Her *Sparrows* of 1926 was one of the finest things she ever did—a gripping tale of an orphan girl taking care of a group of children hired out to a rascally farmer; but also a no-punches-pulled horror yarn. The climax which shows Mary and her young wards making their way through quicksands and climbing over rotting trees at the foot of which wait hordes

of hungry crocodiles was, and still is, a real thriller.

As for actual thrillers—what breath-taking adventures the 20's had to offer. *The Lost World,* with its dinosaurs and prehistoric monsters, was an eye-popper. There was Lon Chaney, a master of make-up who was also a fine dramatic actor. He is best remembered for *The Hunchback of Notre Dame* and *The Phantom of the Opera;* but, in association with a master director of mystery and the bizarre, Tod Browning, he made a whole series of mysteries and horror yarns for MGM.

Some of the most pleasing films of the twenties were not the big dramatic smashes or the huge spectacles, however. They were simple little romances, slight comedies, and fantasies. These films all had one element that made them outstanding— charm. Sometimes it was present in the script, at other times it was created by the star or the director. But it was there.

Charm isn't a quality that can be deliberately put into a film. It has to come by itself. It is the gift of people who love the film they are making and want to pass that feeling along to the people who will see it. It also has to be the result of unhurried, careful film-making.

Many delicate scenes in silent movies came off so well because the makers were willing to work until they were just right. One magnificent moment in *Sparrows* depends for its entire effect on the peaceful and almost happy movement an

ill child makes in the moment of his dying. No matter how talented the child player, it was a scene that could never really be "acted." Mary Pickford, her director William Beaudine and cameraman Charles Rosher might have sat around patiently for hours taking the scene over and over, until either through inspiration or accident the right "take" was obtained. Today such a method wouldn't be possible or financially practical. The set would be cluttered with hairdressers, assistant cameramen, electricians, etc., all of them chafing at delays, and all getting overtime pay. But while production costs were rising in the twenties, they weren't yet astronomical. The absence of sound equipment kept a lot of the cost down, and the stars, often their own producers, really cared about giving, and getting, the very best.

The peak of charm was reached with two adaptations in 1924 and 1925 of stories by James Barrie. Both were directed by Herbert Brenon, and both starred Betty Bronson. The first was *Peter Pan,* in which Betty was exactly right as the boy who never grew up. Blithe and cheerful one moment, downcast and sad the next, her Peter Pan was a wonderful creation. It was all the more remarkable because she had previously played only a handful of bit roles. Actually *Peter Pan* left something to be desired as a film; it didn't take full advantage of the motion picture medium to exploit the magic of Barrie's story. But

A Kiss for Cinderella most certainly did. Even without Betty Bronson's touching performance, it would have been a masterly film, alive with the magic gaiety and tender sadness Barrie gave his original story. One of the greatest (and most neglected) films of movie history, it deserves to be seen again and again.

Betty Bronson, like D. W. Griffith, was a casualty of her times. Audiences had little time to spare for whimsy and fairy tales; they were more interested in the snappy adventures of Clara Bow, or the flapper-age Cinderella of Colleen Moore.

One more great star of the twenties was one of quite another kind, Rin Tin Tin, a handsome wonder-dog with expressive eyes. He could really act. Confronted with complex problems, he would think things over, look to his master for advice, and show puzzlement, sorrow, frustration, love, and indecision in his lovable face. Two of his best silents, *The Night Cry* and *Tracked by the Police,* are ample proof of this. The last one can be seen occasionally on television, and in it the dog not only acts more competently than all the humans on the screen, but works overtime to thwart the villains and single-handedly save a mighty dam from destruction!

By the mid-twenties, however, even such a star as Rin Tin Tin did not prevent the problems from building up. Boxoffice receipts were falling off. In spite of the fact that good pictures outnumbered the bad, and 1925, considered a bad year, produced more good pictures than some recent decades, the public seemed to be losing interest in the movies. The radio was blamed, as television was blamed later. Movies had to seek a new way to compete, and they did. Before the end of the decade, movies had learned to talk. But even this did not solve what was really the basic problem—the slow decline in overall film quality.

Erich von Stroheim directing Gibson Gowland and Zazu Pitts in **Greed**

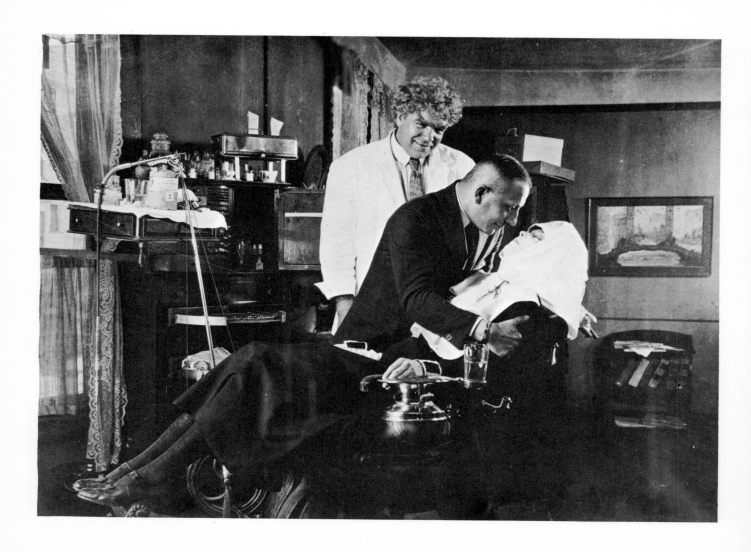

Betty Bronson in **Peter Pan**

Greed
(Director: Erich von Stroheim)
With Gibson Gowland,
Zasu Pitts, Jean Hersholt

Phantom of the Opera
(Director: Rupert Julien)
With Lon Chaney,
Mary Philbin, Norman Kerry

The Big Parade
(Director: King Vidor)
With John Gilbert,
Renee Adoree, Karl Dane

The Lost World
(Directors: Harry Hoyt and Willis O'Brien)
With Lewis Stone, Bessie Love,
Wallace Beery

If any one kind of film stood out above all others in the twenties—both in numbers made and in quality—it was comedy. It is a matter of fact, and not mere opinion, that those years were America's "golden age" as far as movie comedy is concerned.

Audiences, surrounded by post-war problems, wanted to laugh. And the movies catered to their desire. Ideas in comedy that had been born only a few years before were developed, polished, and handled in a dozen different ways. There were scores of comic stars in the twenties; everybody was making short comedies. Many of these pictures were dreadful; but they were soon forgotten, and their stars passed on to an obscurity they deserved. As for the rest, they left ten years of fun that covered every conceivable kind of humor, from slapstick to satire.

The comedies of these years were great at least partly because there was time to make them great. Buster Keaton or Harold Lloyd only needed to turn out one or two pictures a year, in contrast, for example, with the modern T.V. comedian who must turn out a show every week. The old comedians could take their time. They could experiment, retaining only the best ideas and discarding hundreds of gags that might be funny but weren't "the best," and thereby make comedy of a quality that has never been equalled.

Another reason for the greatness of these silent comedies is that their producers were never afraid to take a chance with unusual or offbeat humor. Movie comedies made fun of everybody and everything, themselves most of all. Racial minorities? Jews, Negroes, Poles, Britishers, Italians—all came in for some pretty sharp barbs. So did politicians and bankers, priests, and tax collectors. No subject was immune. The beauty of this was that with everybody and everything being laughed at, nobody was really being singled out. Everybody laughed at everybody else, and it was a healthy state of affairs. The comedies of course, were not funny just because they used this kind of material, but because when something was truly funny and fit the situation, the comedy-makers were free to use it.

Although it's always a little unfair to generalize and to separate movies into neat little packages, one can to a certain extent say that the comedies of the twenties fall into about four groups.

First, there were the purely slapstick shorts made by such producers as Mack Sennett and Hal Roach. Most of these starred comedians like Ben Turpin, Snub Pollard, and Billy Bevan, actors with pleasing personalities who were often very funny, but who didn't really create comedy themselves. They always depended on the quality of their stories and their directors. Thus one Ben Turpin comedy could be hilarious and the next one terribly dull and unimaginative.

On the whole, the two-reel comedies produced by Mack Sennett and Hal Roach did reach an extremely high standard. Other directors like Frank Capra and George Stevens, both then just starting out in movies, also worked on some excellent ones. These comedies provided a wonderful training ground for actors, directors, and cameramen. They offered freedom for the imagination and also had to be made quite cheaply. Working on them was fun, but it was also a good school. If a man didn't learn how to put a movie together efficiently and quickly from working on two reel comedies (or from working on cowboy movies) then the chances were that he would never amount to much in movies.

No one ever demanded that these short comedies follow any rules of logic. The rule was "seeing is believing." If something could be shown on the screen that looked real, it didn't matter how absurd it really was. An automobile could be crushed between two streetcars and still lurch away on four wheels, even though squashed flat as a pancake. A man could be pushed off a high cliff, fall thousands of feet, land on his head, and get to his feet with an angry shake of his fist. Ingenious trick photography, and more often extremely daring work by comedians who permitted themselves to be manhandled or suspended off buildings or cliffs, made all of this look wonderfully real. And it

Reginald Denny
and Laura LaPlante:
Skinner's Dress Suit

Ernst Lubitsch

was all helped by the silence of the movies themselves. The lack of sound seemed to create a barrier that told audiences, even though they didn't know it, "this is a world of comedy—an unreal world all its own."

The second group of comedies were an offshoot of the popular Douglas Fairbanks films of pre-1920. They were the action-comedy-romances, with a likeable breezy hero facing everyday problems with confidence and courage. Reginald Denny starred in some of the best of these. He had a wonderful flair for them. The best were *California Straight Ahead* (dealing with a cross-country cruise by car and trailer, a very popular pastime in the twenties, and winding up with a rousing auto race) and *Skinner's Dress Suit* (a film about the difficulties of a young married couple). None of these films were classics, but they were well made, very popular, and highly profitable.

Third came the group that we can call "sophisticated comedies." These came into being in the mid-twenties, largely as a result of certain European films and the work of such directors as Ernst Lubitsch. They featured situations that were anything but everyday, and their characters were offbeat and worldly-wise. The first of these comedies were overpraised, perhaps because visual and slapstick gags were so common. Films like *The Marriage Circle* offered wit instead of slapstick, and the critics and the public liked them. Strangely, critics

raved over the first films in the cycle, and then, when they, too, had become familiar, ignored some of the best. One of Mary Pickford's last silents, *My Best Girl,* was a delightful blend of comedy of this type with her own more spirited humor. Yet the critics ignored it, and today it is forgotten.

For all of this, however, it is the fourth category of comedy that people really think of when they talk of comedy in the twenties. This is the comedy of the four big producer-stars: Charlie Chaplin, Buster Keaton, Harold Lloyd, and to a lesser degree Harry Langdon. Each was so different in style, and so important, that he is in a sense a category all by himself. But to those who watched them, they were one laughter-producing brotherhood.

Langdon really was, perhaps, in some respects one of the greatest of them all. But unlike the others, he never quite understood just what his appeal was. He could not both produce and direct his own films successfully as the others did. It was other directors, especially Frank Capra, who knew how to handle the strange little screen character Langdon had worked up. This was the character of an overgrown baby—completely trusting, innocent, honest, yet with a certain slyness and guile, too. It was one of the most unique of all comic styles, and Langdon made some marvellous comedies using this adult "baby." Like the others, he knew the value of slapstick, al-

though he, like they, had graduated to a subtler kind of humor. He made up some hilarious situations—a tornado climax for *Tramp Tramp Tramp,* and an episode in *The Strong Man* wherein the meek little hero, posing as a circus strong man, somehow manages to wreck a whole saloon. But his real genius lay in his pantomime. *The Strong Man* also contained a whole ten-minute sequence in which Langdon pantomimed the discomfort of a man with a heavy head cold. His was a wistful and fragile appeal. His delicate combination of comedy and pathos had to be handled just right, or it collapsed. Frank Capra knew how to handle it, but after three successes in a row, Langdon wanted to work entirely on his own. He turned to writing and directing his own films, as well as producing them, and failed. His pictures became forced and unfunny; his popularity dwindled; and the saddest thing of all is that until his death in the mid-1940's he never knew quite what had gone wrong.

The other three comedians had happier careers. Successes from the start, their popularity increased with each picture; and, in varying degrees, they all made successful changeovers to sound films. Charlie Chaplin, of course, is regarded as the undisputed comedy king, a title open to question since he certainly wasn't the funniest of the comedians. But as star-writer-producer-director he was probably the most accomplished; and he unquestionably had the best dramatic sense.

Chaplin's most successful films were made in the twenties, *The Gold Rush, The Kid.* But his best and funniest films were those he made in the 1916–1919 years, and those that he made after 1930. Nevertheless his lovable "little tramp" with the bowler hat, baggy pants, and jaunty cane was probably the most popular single figure on the screen in the 1920's.

Harold Lloyd, like Ben Turpin, Billy Bevan and Snub Pollard, wasn't really funny in himself. He depended on scripts and elaborate gags. But unlike the others, he didn't adopt the guise of a clown. (They all used funny moustaches, unrealistic costuming, and in Turpin's case, cross-eyes.)

Lloyd was a good judge of comedy. His situations involved the climbing of buildings, chases, elaborate slapstick and acrobatic feats. His screen character wanted to be a go-getter but usually didn't have quite enough confidence or intelligence to make it on his own. Finally, more because of the goodness of his heart than because of any real ability, he always won through to success, promotion, and the girl's hand in marriage.

In terms of laugh content, Lloyd's pictures were among the funniest films the twenties produced. And if Lloyd must be considered a likeable and expert manufacturer of comedy rather than a creator, it is no slur. His pictures may have been constructed by an almost mathematical formula; but if they were, they automatically included that which was "sure fire" and eliminated the rest. And the formula paid off. The success drive of Lloyd's bespectacled hero transferred itself to Lloyd personally. A notable success in all his undertakings, Lloyd became a millionaire many times over.

Of the four great comedy stars, Buster Keaton may have been the best of them all—although he was hardly the most popular. Keaton's screen character was far more complicated than Chaplin's or Lloyd's. It wasn't necessary to understand his character to enjoy his films, which were full of rich and original humor, but it was necessary to understand the character to enjoy the pictures fully. Keaton had a sharp, dry wit, a kind of humor rare on the silent screen; rare, in fact, on the screen at all. As a result, his comedies were so fresh and inventive that they still seem ahead of their time.

Keaton's screen character was that of an eternal pessimist. He expected everything to go wrong, and it usually did. When, by a lucky break, something worked out right for him, he was neither surprised nor elated. He just took it in his stride, knowing that the law of averages would soon mess things up again. He was a nice young man, trying to get along in the world, but unlike Lloyd, he didn't try too hard. He ambled along in a dream-like state, never really part of the world; and when he finally achieved success, it was usually due to some lucky break that he probably didn't even know about.

Like Lloyd, Keaton usually had to prove himself to his girl friend—except that his girl friend didn't really care and hardly seemed to know he existed. When she turned him down, he shrugged his shoulders and bided his time. The audience knew he would ask her to marry him again—and she'd turn him down again—but he'd keep trying. There was never any self pity in Keaton; he never cried over his misfortunes, nor did he expect his audience to. Perhaps that was the "common touch" he lacked, which made Chaplin popular and caused audiences to overlook Keaton.

Keaton poked cold and unemotional fun at many of the traditions of screen comedy and especially at the traditional heroine. To most comedians the heroine was sweet and innocent, lovable and intelligent, someone to be cherished and protected. Keaton's heroines usually weren't. They were stupid and generally not very pretty. In a moment they could wreck something he had worked on for hours or days. They weren't worth all the care he gave them, and when they finally consented to marry him, it was partly because no one else would bother to ask them.

This treatment of heroines was just a small facet of the Keaton personality. His most notable trait was his never-ending war with the mechanized world. Everything mechanical seemed designed to defeat him—whether it was a simple deck

chair, a cannon, a locomotive, or an ocean liner. It never really did defeat him, because he always found a solution; but it was the kind of solution that a man from Mars would arrive at— someone discovering the world's problems for the first time and bringing completely foreign ideas to bear upon them.

Keaton's comedies offered some of the most spectacular slapstick sequences and some of the simplest bits of panto- mime. He could get the same huge laughs whether he was standing alone with a couple of simple props and reacting with his usual unsmiling face or was, as in *The General,* getting mixed up in a huge-scale Civil War battle.

The twenties were so rich in great comedy that although "the big four" loom large, they were not all there was. Larry Semon, for example, was a little man with a rather unlovable personality. His films probably got more laughs per foot than anybody's. They were nothing but slapstick. There was no rousing of pity, no subtlety. But there was such speed, such gusto, such expert timing that audiences were breathless. Afterwards, they probably went home and forgot all about it; but they laughed while they saw it. In terms of the energy he put into his films, and the discomfort he must have endured (he was forever undergoing ferocious falls, or tumbling into vats of whitewash or other goo), Semon was the hardest work- ing of all screen comics.

Another fine one was Charlie Chase. Chase had a lovable, breezy screen personality. Some of his films contained excellent slapstick, others were purely situation comedies; but his likeable manner dominated them all. His screen character, in fact, was a little like Lloyd's, except that he was usually smarter. Lloyd got ahead on the theory that he was a nice guy and you can't keep a nice guy down. Chase got ahead because he was a nice guy and had ability, even though it took people a long time to realize it. A master of the art of embarrassment, he was forever being humiliated and caught in situations where the evidence made him look guilty even though he wasn't.

It was Chase's misfortune that he reached his peak a little too late, when the screen was so full of comedians that his only outlet was two reel comedies. But for audiences, this was no tragedy. Instead of a handful of "prestige" features, they had dozens of delightful two-reelers to watch.

No consideration of screen comedy in the twenties is complete without a reference to Laurel and Hardy. Although both had been in comedies since the early days, they didn't get together as a team until 1926. They were an instant hit, realized right away that they worked well together, and decided to stay together.

Laurel and Hardy were the last really classic comedians. Jack Benny, Bob Hope, and others that followed, were primarily dialogue and situation comedians, with their roots in vaudeville and radio. The Marx brothers brought brilliant and insane humor to the screen, but they needed noise, confusion, situations, props. They couldn't just stand on a bare set and be hilarious of themselves, the way Laurel and Hardy could.

Laurel and Hardy are recognized as being among the greats of American comedy. It isn't too much of an exaggeration to say that they belong on the same plane as Chaplin, Keaton, Langdon, and Lloyd. And in the realm of comedy creation, they are really surpassed only by Keaton. They worked wonderfully as a team, both in front of and behind the camera. Hardy was the cleverer performer, although it was to Laurel that the bulk of the comedy fell. Hardy was actually a fine actor and could have been a successful dramatic actor if he had not decided to make people laugh instead. Laurel, the blank-faced goof, forever devoid of intelligence and whose few good ideas always go awry, was quite the opposite in reality. His was the creative mind behind most of the comedies. It was he who dreamed up many of the stories and side-splitting routines. Laurel and Hardy were the only comedy team in which one member was not just a stooge; they were a perfect unit.

However, because they made so many films, turned out on an almost assembly-line basis, some of what they did was inferior. And so, recognition of their talents came late—so late, in fact, that Oliver Hardy had already died, and Stan Laurel, ill and in retirement, was unable to be more than gratified by the honors heaped upon him.

The Laurel and Hardy films were deceptively simple in theme, and were put together quite precisely—sometimes a little too precisely. The films built steadily, like a baby building a tower with bricks, and then, finally, all the bricks were sent toppling in a final burst of frenzy. Quite often they would take a single situation and make a whole film of it. *Big Business,* for example, one of their silent classics, has them trying to sell Christmas trees in July to reluctant Californians. One householder, played by their regular enemy James Finlayson, gets violent. He chops up their tree with a pair of shears, thinking this will get rid of them. But it is only the start. Laurel takes a penknife and pries loose the numbers from Finlayson's front door. He retaliates by ripping Hardy's shirt and breaking his watch. From then on, the violence mounts in ever-increasing fury. The boys rip out Finlayson's telephone and heave it through a window. He smashes the windshield on their car. At the end of two hilarious reels, his lovely home is a complete shambles; windows broken, doors smashed, chimney destroyed, the rooms soaked by a gardening hose, and the garden looking like a battlefield. Finlayson for his part has successfully wrecked Laurel and Hardy's business by destroying their only

assets—the Christmas trees and their car, which he has systematically pulled apart, blown up, and hammered into wreckage.

Violence of this sort was an integral part of the Laurel and Hardy comedies. It was vicious, even cruel, yet somehow acceptable because it was unreal. The victim of all this destruction never interfered in his own defense or in the defense of his property. He stood by watching, with a sort of detached interest, while the boys did their worst. Then it would be his turn, and Laurel and Hardy, like true gentlemen, stood back while he went to work. All their wild orgies of destruction had this elements of organization and the hint of gentlemanly sportsmanship behind the temporary, uncontrollable anger.

Hardy was a joy to watch—ultra-gallant, over-pompous, yet not annoyingly so, full of elegant flourishes, determined to conduct himself like a prince even though he might be clothed in rags. His performances contained some striking new things: most effective of all, the direct appeal to the audience. Let Hardy be subjected to some extreme form of violence—falling down a chimney perhaps, or having a piano fall on top of him —and it would be followed by a full close-up of him staring with resignation at the audience. He invited, almost demanded, pity and understanding not only for his immediate situation but for the future disasters that were bound to come from his association with "my friend Mr. Laurel."

Few stars over the years have given audiences more pleasure and genuine, hearty laughter, than Laurel and Hardy. But for years, while adults often found them hilarious (but dismissed them as "silly") and the critics took no notice at all it was the children alone who not only loved them, but somehow understood them much better as well.

Laurel and Hardy

Why Worry?

Hot Water

THE COMING OF SOUND

Roughly speaking, the coming of the talkies coincided with Lindbergh's solo flight across the Atlantic in 1927. The two events seemed to herald a new age of mechanical marvels, and, some thought, great changes in public taste. One movie critic, praising Lindbergh's achievement, promised that this would be the end of the cowboy as a movie hero. The aviator was the new hero, he said, and Ken Maynard and Buck Jones had better take to the air if they wanted to survive. The airman hero was popular for a while, and has now been replaced by the astronaut; but the cowboy is still as popular as ever. Similarly, another critic, enthusiastically reporting on one of the first sound films, stated that no one would ever look at a silent film again; that the worst sound film would always be preferable to the best silent. Actually, some of the early talking films now seem far more like museum pieces than the silents they were replacing.

Sound had been a long time coming to the movies. There had been many experiments, from the earliest days on. Edison had, by 1915, developed a fairly workable system involving a phonograph disc played in synchronization with the film. Copies of these films which exist today show that the sound was crude but adequate, and doubtless could have been improved on with further experimentation. But because Edison never used his device dramatically, his sound films remained a mechanical

novelty limited to vaudeville-like acts only.

D. W. Griffith used sound in the early twenties for a sequence in a picture called *Dream Street*. But the initial interest in this was never followed up.

In the late twenties Warner Brothers were persuaded to take a chance on another sound system—the system that came to be known as Vitaphone. It was something like the Edison method, for it used a disc that had to be run in synchronization with the film. Such a system has one obvious limitation: if a film should be damaged, and a torn or otherwise spoiled section be removed, which can often be done without any noticeable change in the picture itself, the matching up of sound is automatically lost. Engineers realized this, but before overcoming it decided first to prove that sound films could be commercially successful.

The first Vitaphone program was presented in 1926. The main feature of the evening was *Don Juan*, a cloak-and-dagger romance with John Barrymore. The sound was limited to an elaborate musical score, performed by the New York Philharmonic, and to such sound effects as swords clashing and horses' hooves galloping. But the rest of the program included a number of short subjects in which speech and singing were added to the music. Surprisingly, no one was too excited about the possibilities of speech and song. Because the shorts were nov-

elty items, their sound was dismissed as a novelty, too.

Even the Warner studio didn't realize what had been done. It wasn't until the following year that they made *The Jazz Singer* with Al Jolson. Most of this picture was made as a silent, with the dialogue and other explanatory text written in titles. The sound came in the musical score, and Jolson sang several songs. In addition, he also delivered a few lines of dialogue. Jolson's magnetic personality and the enthusiasm with which he launched into his songs had an almost magical effect. Instantly, the power and appeal of talkies was apparent. That *The Jazz Singer* was basically a silent film, and an extremely good one, has been forgotten. It is remembered as the film that made talking pictures popular.

Almost immediately the industry was in another upheaval. Warner Brothers followed with the first all-talking film, a gangster film called *Lights of New York* which was an enormous success. But it did not promise well for the artistic future of pictures. It was slow, badly acted and directed, and lacked the fine photography and other artistry of *The Jazz Singer*.

All of the big companies switched to programs of sound pictures at once. The big silent hits from previous years were hurriedly brought back and fitted out with musical scores and sound effects. New pictures that had been made as silents were likewise given musical scores and effects; and usually one or

two lengthy talking scenes were filmed and clumsily inserted. Often the balance of the whole film was upset and sometimes the picture was completely ruined; but it could be advertised as "part talkie." Even the great silent film *White Shadows in the South Seas* was sold as a sound film on the basis of a short scene in which the hero taught the island-girl heroine to whistle.

Soon, even the phrase "part-talkie" indicated an outdated film, and the audience-attracting slogan became "100% All-Talking, All-Singing." Many of the smaller companies, unable to afford the expensive changeover to new equipment, went out of business. And the small movie houses, too, found themselves faced with problems. It cost money to convert their theaters to sound, and there was the added problem that not all of the movie producers were using the same sound system. Warners had the system of discs; Fox, on the other hand, was using the system that is in use today—recording the sound right on the film itself. Because of these problems, the transition from silent films to sound took a long time. Silents and talkies played side by side. Companies issued their more important films in both silent and sound versions. And for three whole years the silent movie was slowly dying.

But if it was dying, it was doing so gallantly. Some of the biggest stars—John Barrymore, Douglas Fairbanks, Gloria

Swanson—made spectacular "last stands" in silent films that
went into production long after it was clear that talkies had
come to stay. For talkies had one serious drawback: the camera was a captive of the sound equipment. If the camera moved,
the microphones either picked up too much noise or failed to
work properly. Rather than take time out to solve these problems, directors stopped their cameras from moving. All of the
old movie grammar that Griffith had pioneered was thrown
overboard. Films were shot in long static takes; editing was at
a minimum; camera movement became almost non-existent.

The silents that were still being made—films like John Barrymore's *Tempest* or Corinne Griffith's *The Garden of Eden*—
took advantage of their temporary superiority in technique
and became elaborate examples of what could be done. The
sets gleamed and glistened; the cameras glided, swung, danced;
trick effects ran riot. But the more elegant and pictorially expert these films were, the more antiquated they seemed. The
new fashion was for talk, sound, noise; and nothing seems more
out-of-date than the fashion of only yesterday.

Not all of the final silents were of this overlavish variety,
however. One silent of 1928, *The Crowd,* directed by King
Vidor, is almost certainly one of the ten finest films ever made.
It achieved its greatness not through a display of technique,
but through simplicity, honesty, and understatement. Al-

Sunrise:
George O'Brien
and Margaret Livingston

though audiences of 1928 were not interested in this sensitive, true picture of the joys and sorrows of a very ordinary couple, it is a film that is honored the world over today.

Equally honored is another silent of just the year before, *Sunrise*. The first American film of the German director F. W. Murnau, it can be called "a film poem." These two pictures were both made at a time when it was obvious that such "art-for-art's sake" productions would not pay off at the boxoffice. It is to the credit of the industry that they could be made, and were made.

Not only did the mechanics of the movies change with sound, but for a long time the content changed, too. The comedies abandoned their slapstick and began to talk instead. Limited to stage skits and situation comedies based on error and misunderstanding, they soon became tiresome and boring. The old serial thrillers, too, were never quite the same. Serials continued until the mid-1950's, but the spirit was gone. Sound added a dimension of realism that now made them seem absurd.

Since sound was the thing, there was a sudden rush to musicals and the filming of novels and plays. Each studio made at least one All-Star revue using all their top actors. Some of the musicals used the newly developing Technicolor, also. But they were static films, little more than photographed stage shows.

The cameras did not get up close to the singers, or move with the dancers.

Many of the dramas based on plays or novels did literally nothing but talk. Even when there was a logical plot excuse for action, it was often only talked about and not shown. Some of these films had a strong star, perhaps from the stage, who was a good actor or actress and worth watching and listening to; but most of them just talked, talked, talked.

There were film-makers of vision, however, who refused to throw away the style they had acquired. Somehow, they were determined to overcome the purely mechanical problems involved. And in 1929, a number of films began to appear in which the camera did move again, in which the absence of sound was used as dramatically as its presence.

Most notable of all was a film called *Applause*. It was directed by a man named Rouben Mamoulian, who had never made a picture before. His previous experience had been on the stage. Mamoulian, not knowing what couldn't be done, refused to believe it when his cameramen and sound technicians told him, "You can't do it that way," or "This won't work." Mamoulian insisted—for a while earning the enmity and contempt of most of the crew—and finally came up with a remarkable film. It had a flowing pictorial style and an interesting way of blending picture and sound. He took his cameras out into the

New York streets and subways and to the Brooklyn Bridge, although outdoor shooting was rare in this period because of the mechanical difficulties involved.

Films like *Applause* and one by King Vidor called *Hallelujah,* a moving and exciting picture about a Negro community in the South, which used sound well, were not especially successful. Because they were not dominated by sound, there were those who called them old-fashioned. But they were important not only because they were fine films, but because they showed other directors that they could get away from their static styles.

To fully grasp the daring of a film like *Applause* one has only to contrast it with *The Canary Murder Case,* made the same year by the same company. It was a Philo Vance murder mystery in which all the detective work was performed in long, long dialogue scenes. The camera never moved. The identity of the killer was obvious from the beginning, and the only real excitement for the audience was in trying to spot where the director had hidden the microphones to pick up the dialogue. This turned into quite an amusing game. A bowl of flowers, placed in most unlikely surroundings, or an unusually thick telephone that always seemed to be right in front of the player speaking, were dead giveaways!

Generally speaking, however, after this initial static trial

period was over, most film-makers and film actors survived the change-over to sound quite well. Some top directors, like John Ford, found that sound gave them added advantages for emotional appeal or for acting subtleties, and went on to make their greatest pictures.

Despite legends to the contrary, only a few stars found themselves defeated by poor voices. Most of the top stars—Greta Garbo, Harold Lloyd, Gloria Swanson, Douglas Fairbanks, Mary Pickford—made the transition with ease. The comedies of Laurel and Hardy, for example, gained tremendously from the pompous, flowery language of Hardy, and the infantile simperings of Laurel. John Barrymore's rich voice and stage training made him a spectacular success. Within the first few years of sound films, he made a great array of pictures, covering the whole range of melodrama, tragedy, comedy, and drama.

The only big stars who really failed were those whose day was about over anyway. What happened is that the kind of films these stars specialized in—the elaborate romances and costume dramas—were no longer being made. Had Rudolph Valentino, the great lover of the twenties, lived (he died in 1926) his career would most certainly have faded at this time, as did the career of John Gilbert, another romantic hero. But the end came not because of sound but because of a decided change in movie fashions.

The majority of the stars and directors were joined by new blood from the stage—Rouben Mamoulian, Paul Muni, James Cagney. The transition was slow, clumsy, costly. But by the end of 1930, it had been made. In 1930, D. W. Griffith was voted the best director of the year for his *Abraham Lincoln,* a sound film. And also in 1930, one of the classic war films was produced, *All Quiet on the Western Front.* The movies were beginning to move again.

All Quiet on the Western Front
(Director: Lewis Milestone)
With Lew Ayres
Louis Wolheim, Raymond Griffith

THE THIRTIES

Few films have reflected so well the times in which they were made as did those of the thirties. The depression was at its height. The public, unsure of the future and caught in a drab, unexciting, workaday world, wanted and needed escape. Hollywood filled that need in some obvious ways and in some surprising ways, too.

The obvious ways were the ultra-cheerful films: the elaborate musicals, the crazy comedies. Warner Brothers in particular pioneered the "monster-musical" boasting huge production numbers staged by Busby Berkeley. These numbers, according to the plot of the stories, were all supposed to take place on normal-sized theater stages before theater audiences. But as soon as the scene started, the cameras zoomed in and the stages expanded to cover acres of ground. Fleets of taxicabs, hundreds of extras, horses, platoons of chorus girls, elephants, gigantic swimming pools, ten-story buildings, armies of grand pianos all moving on wheels, and battleships would parade in front of the astonished audience. One moment they would be looking at a line of chorus girls singing a song in a speeding locomotive; the next, they'd be concentrating on a bird in its nest or peering through a window at action taking place across the street.

Berkeley designed and edited these sequences with real imagination. He used camera cranes up in the rafters to look

down on chorus girls weaving fantastically elaborate floral patterns. How the supposed theater audience, not perched on the ceiling, was expected to get the benefit of these gyrations was never explained. Berkeley photographed the dancers from above, below, the sides, and through distorting lenses. However, the songs were all tuneful and hummable, the girls were pretty, and the musicals were all grand fun.

Nor, apart from the musical numbers, were they entirely divorced from reality. *42nd Street,* for example, created a realistic picture of the dog-eat-dog show world, stripping off all the glamor and showing it as a hard, ruthless business, as much affected by the depression as anything else.

America needed to laugh in those days, and it did. Chaplin made *City Lights,* probably his best picture. Keaton and Lloyd were still active, as were Laurel and Hardy. The Marx Brothers were making their first and best comedies, and W. C. Fields was coming into his own. Depression audiences could appreciate a man who felt he had to cheat to survive; a man who automatically distrusted everyone, the banks especially, and who hated dogs and children. Such Fields classics as *It's a Gift* rank with the very best of Keaton, Langdon, and Chaplin as supreme American film comedy.

One kind of comedy was especially related to the times. This was the modern Cinderella story. Poor, hard-working shop girl sets out to marry a millionaire, falls in love with a nice young man but spurns him because he's poor, and finally accepts him in marriage just before she finds out that he is a millionaire after all. He has proof that she loves him for himself alone; she has a husband and security. Another variation was for the poor to find themselves happy and contented after all, in contrast to the rich, who were beset with problems and often wound up jumping out of windows.

Perhaps as a reaction against the drudgery of day to day living, the so-called "screwball" comedies came into being. They were pictures that said in effect: "Life is miserable and dishonest, so why take it seriously? Laugh at everybody and everything, and things won't look quite so bad." *20th Century,* which made fun of the theatrical world and starred John Barrymore, and *Nothing Sacred,* which lampooned everything from sensational newspapers to the Girl Scouts, were the best examples of these comedies.

Other pictures drew their roots from the depression in a different way. A few films dealt with social problems, films like *I Am a Fugitive from a Chain Gang* and much later *They Won't Forget,* which told the story of a lynching in a southern town. These not only explored important themes, but, in a way, were as comforting as comedy. They seemed to tell audiences: "Look how much worse things could be; look at the fix

The Black Cat:
Boris Karloff

Mystery of the Wax Museum:
Lionel Atwill

the depression put these people in; maybe you're not doing so badly after all."

The need for escape expressed itself in still other ways. There was a rebirth of the epic western. *Cimarron* in the early thirties, and *The Plainsman* and *Union Pacific* in the mid-thirties seemed to say that the depression could be licked with a return to the spirit that had inspired the western pioneers. There was a boom in travel films and jungle adventures that were designed to relieve the cooped-up feeling created by the depression. And as often happens in times of gloom and worry, there was a big cycle of horror movies.

The horror movies of the early thirties were grim, carefully made, expensively produced. In contrast to today's horror films, they kept gore, blood, and unpleasantness to a minimum. They achieved their results by mood, atmosphere, and a subtle undercurrent of horror. *Dracula* and *Frankenstein* were the films that started the cycle, but they both suffered from comparatively crude production. They had style, but little polish. Later films like *The Mummy, The Black Cat* and *The Mystery of the Wax Museum* showed great improvement, as did *King Kong,* the greatest depression-era horror movie of them all. It combined the three most important elements for a movie in those days: the Cinderella story (the heroine, starving, resorting to stealing apples, is rescued from a soup kitchen by the

The Mummy

Dames: A Busby Berkeley musical

hero and immediately turned into a movie star); the escapism of jungle adventure; and the monster-menace.

These horror films made stars of Boris Karloff, Bela Lugosi and Lionel Atwill. James Whale became the master director. *The Bride of Frankenstein* which he made in 1935 can still be considered the classic film in the horror/science fiction class.

In spite of a general lack of money that invaded even the movie studios, some courageous films were made in the early years of the thirties. Josef von Sternberg did a series of lush, extravagant films with Marlene Dietrich as his star. They lauded her beauty in particular and the purely pictorial elements of films in general. *Morocco, Dishonored, The Shanghai Express, Blond Venus,* and *The Scarlet Empress* and *The Devil Is a Woman* all followed the same pattern. They either had no stories at all or had stories so silly they were absurd. But they were stunning productions to watch. With their huge sets, grotesque decor, gliding camera movements, and breathtaking closeups of Miss Dietrich, they cast a hypnotic spell on the audience.

If there was one element common to most films of the early thirties, especially to those coming from the Warner studio, it was speed and brevity. Two hour films were not uncommon. But it is amazing how many big and important films told their stories in seventy minutes or less, and told them well.

The Public Enemy
(Director: William Wellman)
With James Cagney

Top Hat: Astaire & Rogers

Foremost among these rapid dramas were the gangster films: *The Public Enemy, Scarface, Quick Millions* and others. These crackled in speed, and the dialogue was fast and often brilliant. Such films launched new stars like James Cagney, Pat O'Brien, Edward G. Robinson, and Chester Morris on long "tough guy" careers and established William Wellman, Howard Hawks, Mervyn LeRoy and Rowland Brown as top directors in the field.

But the melodramas began to get a little too tough, the comedies a little too free, the dramas a little too far from what many people considered acceptable. Fearing government or other outside censorship, the industry decided to make its own rules governing controversial matters.

Nineteen thirty-three was the last year of the anything-for-a-laugh, let's-take-a-chance school of thought. By 1934 Hollywood was shifting its gears, and by 1935 it was cruising along a new road. The appeal was now to "The American Family." And Hollywood somehow saw that family as rather dull, a family that wanted to be entertained but didn't want to think and certainly didn't want to be shocked or offended.

Much that came out of this kind of thinking was relaxing and enjoyable. Fred Astaire and Ginger Rogers were enchanting to watch in their big musicals; and Deanna Durbin's glorious voice and sparkling personality were a treat. Will Rogers'

111

Dietrich

homespun humor was pleasing, especially in a comedy like *Steamboat Round the Bend.* Shirley Temple, the greatest and most talented phenomenon since Rin Tin Tin, was rushed through one successful picture after another, never seeming to age. Gene Autry, the singing cowboy, clicked, and there were more singing cowboys to imitate him. But the traditional western seemed to vanish. The horror films petered out. And some of the glamor that had always been a part of movie-making seemed to be gone, too.

The latter part of the thirties did have a few concrete things to offer, however. First: photographically, Hollywood's films had regained the technical perfection that they had lost when the talkies came in. Such middle-thirties films as *The Prisoner of Zenda,* a beautifully done swashbuckler, *Lost Horizon,* offering sound philosophy conveniently sugar-coated in a tale of adventure in Tibet, and the Greta Garbo film *Camille* all offered a polish of production technique not seen for years. Second: the economy policies of the depression were vanishing, and when Hollywood made big adventure pictures, they really made them. The stories, the sets, and the pace were all as good as the production. They delivered all the excitement that the advertising promised. *Mutiny on the Bounty* and *Gunga Din* are two of the best examples of this and among the best examples of the really good films that were made in this period.

As far as new ideas, or really great films were concerned, however, the last years of the decade offered only two striking highlights. First was Walt Disney's first full-length feature, *Snow White and the Seven Dwarfs,* not quite so smooth in its animation as his later films, but easily his best, and of course, *Gone With the Wind.*

It is perhaps unfair to point out that *Gone With the Wind* was not so good a picture as *The Birth of a Nation* and that it is inaccurate in its picture of the Old South. It never set out to be a triumph of film art or a historical document. But as a piece of sure-fire movie-making, it represented the peak of technical brilliance, perfect casting, and absolutely guaranteed boxoffice success.

There have been many better films than *Gone With the Wind* since its release, but no others that have demonstrated so well just what Hollywood can do when all of its resources are brought into play. Its overwhelming success helped to hide the rather barren state of the industry at that time. But if anyone thought it heralded a fresh burst of creative energy, he was only partially right.

Scarface
(Director: Howard Hawks)
With Paul Muni, Karen Morley,
George Raft, Osgood Perkins

Mutiny on the Bounty
(Director: Frank Lloyd)
With Clark Gable, Charles Laughton,
Franchot Tone

THE FORTIES

The forties present a complex, puzzling picture, offering some of the very best and some of the worst of American movies. The blame for many of the poor quality films must be placed on the war. With it, there came a need for light, relaxing, escapist entertainment. The need came first from war workers and from the English market, already involved in fighting the war. Then later it came from the whole American audience: servicemen in camps and overseas, and families at home.

The anxieties were great. The tensions of war work, night shifts, overtime, and headlines, all strong. Hollywood responded with escapism as a steady diet: South Sea island adventures, musicals, comedies.

This was an era of big bands; musicals had less and less story and imagination and more and more concentration on orchestras, singers, and songs. Frank Sinatra, Harry James, Ethel Smith, Tommy Dorsey, Glenn Miller, and Woody Herman were some of the musical personalities who came to the forefront.

With the country in a patriotic fever, dramas and even musicals and comedies were loaded with topical jokes, insults aimed at Hitler and his Axis allies, and a great deal of more-than-obvious propaganda. Today it is almost embarrassing to watch a propaganda sob-story like Ginger Rogers' *Tender Comrade,* or a dull and equally propaganda-soaked musical like *Meet the*

People, a pat on the back for the shipyard workers.

In general, the average film of the forties seems to have dated far more than the average film from any other era. A gentle, minor comedy from the thirties still entertains and appeals today. But many of the comedies from the forties, which seemed fresh and delightful to audiences then, seemed forced and endlessly talkative today.

But, the forties were not all a barren wasteland. Some of Hollywood's more serious directors made a number of pictures that seemed almost ill-timed for such days. Two grim John Steinbeck books, *Of Mice and Men* and *The Grapes of Wrath,* were starters. Both were done with moving beauty and restraint, but were forceful in the message they presented and artistic in style and technique.

Then, John Ford, who made *The Grapes of Wrath,* suddenly, in a burst of astonishing energy, turned out one great film after another. At least two of them, *The Long Voyage Home* and *How Green Was My Valley* were the very opposite of light escapism. William Wellman made a classic and savage study of mob violence, *The Ox-Bow Incident.* And *Citizen Kane,* based on the life of newspaperman William Randolph Hearst, was the most dynamic piece of individual film-making since *Intolerance.* It suggested that Orson Welles, its director, might be to sound films what Griffith had been to silents. But the freedom that such a figure needed no longer existed. Costs

were too high, supervision and control too rigid, and lack of audience demand too great. It is remarkable that Welles was able to make *Citizen Kane* at all.

The war years had a good deal to offer in the way of genuinely creative comedy, too. Laurel and Hardy were making their last films, pale shadows of their former work since slapstick was now frowned upon as outdated, but still good, sound comedy. W. C. Fields made a wonderful recovery from a string of bad films with four comedies that he wrote himself under such names as Mahatma Kane Jeeves and Charles Bogle. Of these, *The Bank Dick* was truly a masterpiece.

The situation comedies were also returning to earlier traditions. The Russians were our allies then, but once again nothing was sacred to comedy-makers. *His Girl Friday* made fine fun out of American Communists; and *Comrade X,* an undeservedly forgotten Clark Gable comedy, had great fun with its conversion of a pretty Communist (Hedy Lamaar) to the ways of democracy.

The real highlight of comedy in the forties, however, was the work of Preston Sturges. He was a familiar writer from the thirties who suddenly blossomed forth at Paramount as a writer-producer-director of some wonderfully original comedies. He had a unique knack of mixing sly satire with the wildest of slapstick. More than anything else he loved to show how

Sullivan's Travels

Gary Cooper

meaningless a slogan like "The American Way of Life" could be, and to expose to ridicule all the things most Americans take seriously, or at least think that they should take seriously. Yet there was often a serious purpose underlining his films, and his hilarious fun was often the sugar-coating on a lot of common sense, pointing up things that really are important. *Sullivan's Travels, The Palm Beach Story* and *Christmas in July* were the best of a long series of these warmly human and richly funny comedies.

The early forties also brought the peak of the star system. The men, however, took something of a back seat. The biggest male stars were Clark Gable, James Cagney, Cary Grant, Gary Cooper and Robert Taylor. Some of them naturally spent a good part of the war years in the armed forces. Newer stars like Kirk Douglas and Burt Lancaster came to take their place, and to offer a less handsome, more rugged kind of leading man. But on the whole, these years were ruled by the ladies, and the few men that were available were shunted into the important pictures. In films like MGM's "Dr. Gillespie" series, every time a door opened, in would come some veteran player like Lionel Barrymore, Walter Kingsford, or Addison Richards, men too old for the army, or some teen-age boy who had not yet been called.

For the ladies, however, it was a field day. Betty Grable, and

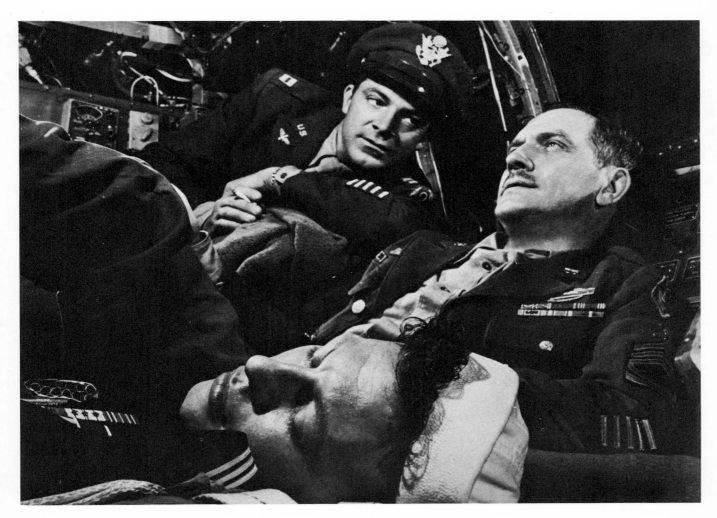

Rita Hayworth kept up the morale of the boys at the front, and Bette Davis, Joan Crawford, Greer Garson, Ingrid Bergman and Ginger Rogers gave some grand-scale soap operas a real boost. Lana Turner, Ann Sheridan, Linda Darnell, Olivia de Haviland, Dorothy Lamour, and Jennifer Jones cheerfully took on westerns, musicals, thrillers, comedies, and whatever else their studios handed them.

In the mid-forties, when the war ended, the movies finally abandoned some of their false gaiety and turned to weightier subjects, or at least to a more realistic treatment. A series of rough, tough, "private eye" thrillers began when Dick Powell abandoned crooning and comedy to play the tough Philip Marlowe in *Murder My Sweet*. A whole group of first-class thrillers followed, rough, tough, and bitingly real. In time these came to follow a formula and the cycle petered out; but similar cycles were ready to replace it.

The Outlaw and *Duel in the Sun* changed the nature of the western. No longer were heroines always virtuous and heroes always to be trusted. A new day had come to the West.

The problems of returning servicemen, as well as the mental problems produced by settling down to life in the post-war world, produced a long series of dramatic films. Servicemen received the best attention in such films as *The Best Years of Our Lives* and *Home of the Brave*. And before the mental problem cycle had worn itself out, there had been an amazing number of heroines who either thought they were going insane, or (as in *The Locket* and *The Snake Pit*) actually were. There were dream sequences designed by surrealist Salvador Dali, melodramas set in mad houses, previously clean-cut heroes such as Robert Taylor appearing as men driven to kill, and an impressive line-up of young men fondly imagining that they were killers when they were not. An offshoot of this trend were the detailed studies of alcoholism: Ray Milland in *The Lost Weekend* representing the men, and Susan Hayward the ladies in the more artificial but still effective *Smash Up*.

Not all of these problem films were great, not all of them were even good. But at least they were a sign that once again Hollywood was trying to grow up and to experiment in new directions. And looking back at the forties, the record isn't really a bad one. Then, as before, there were men willing to take a chance, and people willing to do more than produce just the pictures that would be popular, films that did no more than follow a current trend.

The Best Years of Our Lives
(Director: William Wyler)
With Fredric March, Myrna
Loy, Dana Andrews

Of Mice and Men
(Director: Lewis Milestone)
With Burgess Meredith, Betty
Field, Lon Chaney Jr.

The Grapes of Wrath
(Director: John Ford)
With Henry Fonda, Jane Darwell,
John Carradine

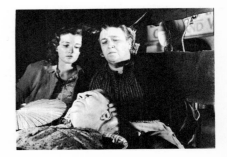

Citizen Kane
(Director: Orson Welles)
With Orson Welles, Joseph Cotten,
Ruth Warwick, George Colouris

The Treasure of Sierra Madre
(Director: John Huston)
With Humphrey Bogart, Walter Huston,
Tim Holt

THE FIFTIES AND EARLY SIXTIES

The fifties and early sixties were less productive of good American films than any other period; and this is a statement that in a very general way can be applied to the films of other countries, too. From 1950 on, it is hard to think of even ten great American films. Defining "great" is, of course, not easy, but probably any film that retains its values through the years, and that thirty years from the date of its production remains not only as enjoyable as it was, but is also as important in theme and as accomplished in a technical and artistic sense, can be considered "great." Such silent films as *Intolerance* and *The Crowd* certainly fall into that class; early sound films like *City Lights, Applause,* and *Trader Horn* do, too. But from the fifties there are only a few that may be well remembered after so long a time has passed. John Ford's *The Wagonmaster* is a good contender, as is Charlie Chaplin's last American film, *Limelight.* Probably two fine films directed by George Stevens, *A Place in the Sun* and *Shane* will live, and also, perhaps, *The Night of the Hunter,* which may be a little too clever and intentionally "artistic" but as least did try to use the camera in a creative way. Not a very large list.

It may be said that, to date, the highest percentage of fine movies were made in the silent era, when the film-makers had more freedom to create. But at that time the tools of film making were not as advanced as they were in the thirties and forties and later. And it is in the 1940's that we find a few films, Orson Welles's *Citizen Kane,* John Ford's *The Grapes of Wrath,* John Huston's *The Treasure of Sierra Madre,* that illustrate sight and sound perfectly welded to produce lasting masterpieces of film art.

But the very complexity of the tools that brought these masterpieces about also prevented more of such films from being made. While a film may legitimately be considered the creation of one man, it is achieved through the combined production efforts of many men. Sets have to be built; a script written; cameramen have to be employed; actors paid; an army of technicians brought into play; complicated and expensive equipment utilized. And when the film is finished in the studio, there are a dozen laboratory procedures to be gone through, to be followed by still more costs in making prints from the negative, in advertising the film, and so on.

A film-maker may spend as little as one hundred thousand or as much as twenty million dollars. The amount expended has little to do with whether the finished product is a masterpiece or not (experience has shown that most of the really great films have been relatively inexpensive ones). But since all films have become more and more expensive to produce, there has been less and less opportunity for the experimenting in the unusual that in the past has brought about such masterpieces as

Citizen Kane or *The Birth of a Nation.*

Although the fifties was a notably empty period in terms of important films, it was a lively period. There were new techniques, new trends in film, new ideas for selling films to the public. And perhaps in these there may lie some value for future generations, as yet undiscovered or undeveloped.

The fifties was the period in which television really caught hold and began to offer serious competition to the movies. The initial impulse of movie-makers was to offer the public films that were bigger and supposedly better than the ones that they could see on television. One of the first results of this was the almost complete elimination of the so-called "B" film—the cheaply-made, second feature, running from an hour to seventy minutes. These had become uneconomical since production costs had risen drastically; and with so many old "B" films on television, there was no great demand for more of them. However, their elimination robbed the screen of such pleasures as the small western (Roy Rogers, Gene Autry and one or two other popular western stars switched to making television westerns, while other old favorites like Johnny Mack Brown, Tim Holt, and Charles Starrett simply retired altogether).

The "B" film had always been a useful training ground for new directors, writers, and stars. Most of the top directors and players had learned the business that way. With this training ground gone, the only place left to learn was television, where production had to be so fast and cheap that there was no time for the newcomer to branch out and try new ideas. The results began to show before too long as new young directors tried to apply the static, talkative methods of TV to the larger screen.

But merely cutting out cheap films and making a few bigger ones like *Quo Vadis?* didn't really help the industry. It needed something radically new, and it seemed to find it in the wide screen. Several new processes were introduced in the early fifties, the most durable of which proved to be CinemaScope. Actually it was not really new; the same process had been used in a number of French films in the twenties and the same shaped screen image had been used constantly by D. W. Griffith. But its wholesale usage, and in color, was new. With its use, however came the usual technical difficulties.

Because of the huge screen area, all the old and effective screen grammar had to be thrown out. Closeups were no longer effective, and vertical action was impossible. In its early days, the images were harsh, fuzzy, and usually out of focus. In time, though, as with changes in the past, its technical flaws were overcome and good directors learned to use the "letter box" shape in such a way that its good points were used to the full and its weaknesses avoided. It was particularly suitable to outdoor subjects, of course, and one of the best westerns of the fifties, *From Hell to Texas,* certainly showed that the new

CinemaScope process could be used creatively.

The one really new innovation in the fifties was the 3-Dimensional film. It was new, that is, in that for the first time it was commercially successful and technically feasible; for 3-D films on a stunt level had existed well back into the silent era. For the first time since sound, a new dimension, that of depth, was brought to the movies; and the fact that the audiences had to wear special glasses in order to see them was only a minor handicap. Unfortunately, the new idea soon died. In order to take advantage of the sudden craze, far too many cheap 3-D films were made. These westerns, horror films, and tropical romances sacrificed the dramatic aspects of depth in favor of the more obvious ones of shock, sensation, and repetitive travel vistas. Too, to gain maximum effect, the 3-D films depended on flawless projection, since two prints of the same film had to be shown at the same time in perfect synchronization. Projection in theaters in the fifties was incredibly sloppy; and if projectionists couldn't keep a normal film in focus, they were doubly inept with a 3-D film. As a result, the public lost interest in 3-D films. This was a pity because the few really good ones—*Hondo, House of Wax,* and especially *Inferno*—were not only good in themselves, but showed enormous possibilities for the new medium.

As the movies became more and more earnest in their attempts to overcome television, somehow they also became

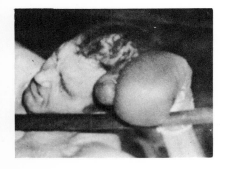

more and more aggressive. It was no longer enough for a thriller to thrill; it had to be rough, tough and savage, too. A film like *99 River Street* went out of its way to include unnecessarily savage beatings; and the advertising proudly informed its audience that it was "like a kick in the teeth." The old gentlemanly heroes were discarded as being too out of touch with the times; now it was fashionable for the "hero" to behave like a lout. He chiseled his way to the top, and somehow audiences were supposed to sympathize with him.

To finance these new ventures, the Hollywood studios sold more and more of their old products to television. But to their surprise, audiences stayed away from the theaters more and more. They stayed home to enjoy the civilized comedy of *The Thin Man* or a Lubitsch film, the charm of Shirley Temple, or the pep of an early thirties comedy like *Blessed Event*. With the new films, one usually had to endure a welter of unpleasant characters, sordid stories, and excessive violence. At home one could relax with the friendly films of the thirties, and the serious films like *I Am a Fugitive from a Chain Gang* which dealt with important social issues without becoming pretentious and violent.

This is not to say that all of the films of the fifties were poor. One of the most pleasing (and little noted) trends was the sudden upswing in the quality of color cartoons. Because they depend so much on technical skills, the animated cartoon is the one kind of film that has improved constantly since its start in 1909. At first the drawings were extremely simple and the dialogue was shown in balloons like newspaper comic strips. But through the years, the cartoons developed a new kind of humor and charm.

Walt Disney was the undisputed leader of the cartoon field in the thirties. He made polished, leisurely cartoons, with more strength in their drawing and in their charm than in their comedy content. But by the fifties, though still the leader in a purely commercial way, Disney had dropped far behind MGM and Warner Brothers. The new cartoons soared with fantastic flights of fancy; their charm may have lessened, but it was replaced by a curiously pleasing, completely and obviously unrealistic, violence.

Actually the new cartoons were reviving the sight-gags of the slapstick two-reelers of the twenties, and they were recapturing that same spirit of boundless fun, too. One can take a silent Mack Sennett comedy like *Yukon Jake,* place it side by side with a Warner cartoon of the fifties (*Lumberjerks*) and find in both films not only identical gags, but the same marvellous disregard for story, logic, and convention so long as the end result is fast and funny.

Many people tend to tar all cartoons by the same brush; to

dismiss them as childish and silly, and admittedly many poor cartoons were made in the fifties—although not by Warners. But one day such cartoons as *One Froggy Evening, Pappy's Puppy* and *Double or Mutton* may be recognized as contributions to the American comedy tradition as great in their way as the contributions of Chaplin or Lloyd.

Another laudable development of the fifties was the far more widespread use of color. Perhaps because it was so widely used, it no longer had quite the same impact as before. In the twenties, a color film like *The Black Pirate* was a rarity. In the thirties, color was still new enough for it to be a drawing card of itself. But by the fifties it was expected, and audiences no longer came just to see color. In fairness, too, it must be said that the color of the twenties and thirties was better because each film was handled in the laboratories with an almost personal care. In the forties and fifties, with color more standardized, it came to be handled on an assembly line basis. Cheaper methods of photographing and processing were found. The result: the average outdoor film of the fifties and sixties (*Cimarron*) could not quite compare with the color quality of a mid-thirties film (*Trail of the Lonesome Pine*).

By the late fifties, the slight edge that the "Wide Screen" had given to the movies was wearing off. Television was catching up again; and the studios came out with the one thing that

television could not duplicate— sheer size. All of the major studios rushed into production with superscale epics (many of them remakes of silent classics) with Biblical or historical themes. At the high production costs prevalent, they were produced at staggering figures. Strangely enough, although most of these films more than paid their way at the boxoffice, they were all quite poor films. *Ben Hur* for example, had nothing to offer apart from the admittedly very exciting chariot race. It was a tediously paced film from a once-dynamic director (William Wyler), and basically it was a cheap-looking film. There were few really big sets, the crowd scenes were routine, and a lot of the apparent bigness was achieved by camera trickery. Yet, somehow the critics were fooled; many rushed into print with claims that this was the biggest spectacle of all. They acclaimed the "great sea battle," evidently taken in by crude little miniature ships tossing about in a tank.

The most annoying thing of all was that so few of the millions of dollars expended on these large, showy films showed up on the screen. A great percentage of the cost went for star salaries, still more to the veritable armies of minor technicians employed by current union requirements. Further, huge sums were diverted to "general studio expenses and overhead," even though most of the films were not made in the home studio at all, but were made abroad in studios that had their own "gen-

eral expenses and overhead." The result: probably less than half of the claimed budget for a picture like *Ben Hur* went to sets or action or other elements of the picture itself. (When Griffith made a spectacle, every cent that he spent showed up in the final picture!)

However, if nothing else, some of the money *Ben Hur* and others like it made perhaps went to finance better pictures. Perhaps some went to pay for a minor classic like the 1962 western *Ride the High Country*.

Hand in hand with the spectacles, came a return of the "B" film, but the "B" film with a difference. Producers found that the only way to make money was to make a very expensive film which cost millions—and could make millions—or to make a very cheap film—so cheap that it could hardly lose money. The result was a never-ending stream of poor taste: cheap spectacles (*Hercules*), cheap horror films (*I Was a Teenage Werewolf*), and cheap juvenile delinquency and exposé films (*College Confidential*). All of these were sold on purely negative qualities; and most of them, thanks to cunning advertising campaigns, went on to far more profits than they deserved. These films claimed to be "adult" and "outspoken," taking advantage of the greater freedom given to the screen.

This freedom came about when the industry decided that if it was to compete with television, it couldn't do so solely by appealing to the eyes and the emotions by way of such "big" films as *Ben Hur* and *The Ten Commandments*. Television, it was argued, was intellectually barren. The movies would supply what television lacked.

Since 1933, when the movies had begun to cater to "the family trade," there had been rigid rules. A film-maker couldn't tackle this subject; there were certain situations that he must avoid; a number of words that he must never use. Somehow, this didn't stop mature films from being made. *The Asphalt Jungle, Of Mice and Men* and *Shadow of a Doubt* managed to be fine films without breaking the code.

But in the fifties, the movies decided to change the rules, to "mature." Problems like drug addiction came off the "tabu" list. Forbidden words became permissible. The screen, film-makers, announced, was grown-up. The result, unfortunately, was a long parade of ugliness and poor taste—a long line of humanity's worst features paraded before the viewing public. Why a person had to be in some way in conflict with the social and moral codes of society to be a believeable "adult" was never explained. In their tasteless dwelling on such areas, the movies actually became as childish and one-sided as if they had reverted to a steady diet of Shirley Temple and Rin Tin Tin. And the results were a good deal less enjoyable.

The early sixties, however, brought signs of unrest; surpris-

David Bradley

Stanley Kubrick

ingly (to Hollywood) comedies began to make as much money as problem pictures, and there was a refreshing return to the long-abandoned comedy field. There were vague experiments in other directions, too. The public, reminded endlessly on TV of what good films really were, showed its weariness of much that was new. Soon theaters found that they could make far more money and satisfy their customers better with the old instead. Obviously films cannot—and should not—live in the past. But there has come increasing recognition that the past is not necessarily dead. Audiences have proved it by their support of the great old films. And some of the younger, more enthusiastic directors, Stanley Kubrick, David Bradley and others, have proved it, too, by studying the film masters of the past and by freely building on what the past accomplished.

The fifties and early sixties were, perhaps, the most unfruitful years in the whole history of movies. But perhaps, too, in their very mistakes they taught lessons that needed to be taught. Perhaps they gave Hollywood, with its wealth of talent and vast reservoir of unmatched equipment, a chance, once more, to shift gears and begin again. As in any art form, there are years of advance, years when new talent and new ideas abound, and years of waiting for the impulses to mature that make such progress possible. Out of what has been, and out of dry years, the future often brings wholly unforeseen advances.

Night of the Hunter
(Director: Charles Laughton)
With Robert Mitchum, Lillian Gish,
Shelley Winters, Peter Graves

Limelight
(Director: Charles Chaplin)
With Charles Chaplin, Claire Bloom, Sidney
Chaplin, Buster Keaton, Snub Pollard